The
KING'S
CUPBOARD

How to Access the King
That is Within You

ELRAY C. TASKER

THE KING'S CUPBOARD
How To Access the King That is Within You
Copyright © 2021 by Elray C.Tasker

Unless otherwise indicated, all scripture quotations, references and definitions are from the Authorized King James Version © 1987; The New King James Version © 1982 by Thomas Nelson, Inc.; The New International Version © 1973, 1978, 1984 by International Bible Society by the Zondervan Corporation; The Amplified Bible Old Testament © 1962, 1964, 1965, 1987 by the Zondervan Corporation; The Amplified New Testament © 1954, 1958, 1987 by the Lockman Foundation; The Message. Copyright © 1993, 1994, 1995, 1996, 2000, 2001, 2002.

Elray C. Tasker
elraytasker72@yahoo.com

ISBN: 978-1-943342-01-3

DestinedToPublish.com | (773) 783-2981

Dedications

This book is dedicated to My Source and My Supply, God/ YHWH/The Most High. Father, without you, not only would this book not exist, but neither would I. To my Lord and Savior Jesus Christ. As long as I have breath, you will get my YES.

To my parents, Donald and Earline Tasker. I owe you more than I can repay. I thank God for choosing you to be my parents, because He knew that everything I needed to become and fulfill His purpose was within you. I love you both.

To my aunt Willie L. Guidry. Your love, mercy, and kindness have been not only my example, but an example to your children, grandchildren, nephews and nieces, and everyone who knows you. Your kindness is immeasurable. You are God's love on this earth.

To My Two Heartbeats, My Inheritances, and my reason for my fight, my son, Daniel, and my daughter, Rayel Jene. You two are the reason that my head rises from the pillow and my feet hit the floor. Although there are more people attached to my purpose than I can imagine, my main purpose is to be your dad, and it's a job and title that I cherish greatly and always will. I love you both with all of my heart!

Acknowledgments

I would first like to thank Apostle Dr. Marshall Davis and Prophetess Catherine Davis for setting me on the path of faith and being examples of godliness before me. As I once told you, "Before I met you, I didn't believe that it was possible to live a Christian life." I thank you for what you have sown into my life personally and spiritually.

I would also like to thank Apostle Dr. Matthew L. Stevenson III. You have stretched and challenged me beyond my limits, and your words and life have provoked me to love God's people past religion and serve them wholeheartedly. Thank you for never trying to "detour me from my destiny." Sir, your pour is immeasurable in my life. Thank you for your "YES" to God.

To all the families that raised me from 79th and Bennett and Euclid, you have been my village. I pray that, in some way, the time you invested in my upbringing was as joyous for you as it was for me, and that this book makes you proud, because it is an example of what you all have shown to me.

Lastly, I would like to thank all the men who aren't mentioned by name in this book but who are the great examples I have written about in these pages. I'd especially like to thank Algean Garner Sr., a.k.a. "Big Gean." What you showed me as a young boy, and the time that you invested in me, is a debt that I can never repay. However, this book is a small tribute to you and men like you who have made me want to serve and live my life in a knightly manner.

Thank you,
Elray Christopher Tasker

Contents

Chapter I: Introduction 1

Definition of a King.. 2

What is a Cupboard? 4

The Purpose of a Cupboard 4

What Should Be in Your Cupboard? 5

Taking Inventory of Your Cupboard 6

How to Fill Your Cupboard..7

    1. What Are Your Perishables? 8

    2. What Are Your Non-Perishables?.............................9

    3. What Are Your Must-Haves and Survival Necessities?........... 15

The Ascension to Kingship..17

    1. Foundational Necessities 19

    2. Growth Acknowledgments 20

3. Understanding Where You Are Deficient 21

Chapter II: Courage **23**

The Man Who Would Be King... 23

1. What Are Kingly Requirements? 24

2. About Your Consorts 27

3. Your Mentors and Trainers... 29

4. How to Enter and Exit.. 30

5. How to Adorn Yourself with Kingly Apparel............................. 31

Fighting Your Dragons.. 34

1. Proper Posture.. 34

2. Selecting Your Weapons of Warfare.. 35

3. Realization of Your Strengths and Weaknesses........................37

4. Strategy for Battle 38

Understanding Your Armor: What Armor Do You Require? 40

1. Is Your Armor Adequate for Your Particular Battle?................42

2. Does Your Armor Fit You?..42

3. Has Your Armor Been Fortified?..45

4. Are There Chinks in Your Armor? 50

What and Who Are You Fighting For?...52

1. What Are the Conditions of Your Battles?.................................. 55

2. Where Are Your Battles Taking You?..57

3. Is Your Battleground a Familiar Place? 59

4. Do You Have a Battle Strategy and Plan for Success? 62

5. Do You Understand Who or What Your Enemy Is?................ 65

6. Are You Acting as Your Own Enemy?...67

Chapter III: Dressing 70

Understanding Why You Dress 70

What Does Your Wardrobe Say About You?................................72

What Is Your Purpose for Dressing? 74

Where Will Your Wardrobe Give You Access To?............................ 76

Are You Dressing for Your Present, or for Your Future?................ 79

Don't Dress Because It's Popular,
    Dress Because It's Purposeful 82

Does Your Dress Inspire or Irritate? 84

Chapter IV: A Seat at the Table 87

What a Seat at the Table Means... 87

What Gives You a Seat at the Table?... 89

What Privileges Does a Seat Give You? 92

What Responsibilities Does a Seat Bring?............................93

Chapter V: Knighthood..................................99

Taking on a New Title 99

    1. Why Is a Title Bestowed? 101

    2. The Requirements of Title Maintenance..................103

    3. Understanding What It Means to Bow and Rise..................106

    4. The Duties of a Knight 108

Chapter VI: Squires 111

Making Squires 111

Selecting Squires: What Makes a Good Candidate?..................113

The Investment Benefits You More Than the Candidate 115

Why Is It Necessary to Make Squires?..............................117

The Life You Live Before Your Squire..............................118

Taking Squires to the Next Level..................................121

The Insurance of Continued Legacy.................................124

Chapter I

Introduction

The mission of *The King's Cupboard* is to create a "Whole Man." The term "Whole Man" is used in reference to the scripture James 1:4-5: *"But let patience have her perfect work, that ye may be perfect and entire, wanting nothing. If any of you lack wisdom, let him ask of God, that giveth to all men liberally, and upbraideth not, and it shall be given him"* (KJV).

The King's Cupboard is designed with the concept in mind, that everything in life, both natural and spiritual, is found and addressed in this book. *The King's Cupboard* is designed to bring into existence the whole man and take him through a step-by-step process to become everything God designed man to be. It is crafted to instill fundamental and foundational truths of manhood that address the needs of men, from dressing to fatherhood, from husbandry to spiritual principles, and from community activism to stewardship. Now, this is not just an initiative for outward growth, but it also addresses the need for building and patience, and it further details the need for staged growth and ascension. The intent of *The King's Cupboard* is to ensure that at the end of the process, true kings and priests are developed, have gone line upon line, and have been prepared unto every good work.

The vision of *The King's Cupboard* is not only to grow a brand, but to instill a culture, and to renew the minds of men not only to think futuristically, but to reestablish principles and fundamentals that will ensure that a legacy is left behind. This legacy will not only shape but grow a heritage of pride, honor, and dignity through precepts and examples of building strong men, and teaching that life is earned and learned in levels.

Definition of a King

Webster's Dictionary provides several significant definitions of a king:

1. A male sovereign or monarch; a man who holds by life tenure, and usually by hereditary right, the chief authority over a country or people.

2. God or Christ.

3. A person or thing preeminent in its class.

4. Chess: The chief piece of each color, whose checkmating is the object of the game; moved one square at a time in any direction.

5. Checkers: A piece that has been moved entirely across the board and has been crowned, thus allowing it to be move in any direction.

These are very revelatory definitions, in my estimation, because not only do they define the natural birthing of one born into the lineage of kingship, but they also give definitions of both the parameters and the strategic authority of a king's reign. These definitions will be revisited in the following segments, but for now, I just needed to show the importance of the initial dictates.

It is very amazing to me that definitions 4 and 5 give such an illuminating reference to a king's purpose in strategic instances as it relates to chess and checkers. You see, both games determine that the king is vitally important in winning. In chess, the game is over when the movement of the king is nullified, and in checkers, when a piece moves across the board, it is crowned king and has unlimited mobility. Such it is, as it relates to life. Your opponent or adversary (I like to say the devil) wants to keep you from your authority by keeping you from moving in your designed power. It's all done step by step, but it's not limited to one direction. As it relates to checkers, you only get crowned king when you have been moved across the board step by step, and then you are granted full reign and have no limit in how or in what direction you move. That's how God designed and desires us to be, but it's only after we complete the steps that we get the authority of unlimited movement.

However, realize that in both games, there is a process before and after kingship is acquired. In checkers, you only get authority after you have gone step by step and have avoided falling prey in battle against your opponent. Then and only then are you awarded kingship, and that's because you have been proven to be wise enough to wield the power and authority that you have been afforded. In chess, it is switched around. It is my belief that chess is the advanced stage of checkers. My thinking is that checkers teaches you how to become king, and chess teaches you how to use your authority over others and move strategically in tearing down your adversary's kingdom.

What is a Cupboard?

The word "cupboard" is an English term, defined by the Cambridge Dictionary as "a piece of furniture or a small part of a room with a door behind which there is space for storing things, usually on shelves." Also, it was originally defined as an open-shelf side table used to display dishware, specifically plates, cups, and saucers. They typically had one to three shelves, and at that time, a drawer or multiple drawers fitted to them.

The Purpose of a Cupboard

The initial purpose of a cupboard was to put things on display, but not to be handled or touched, because they were precious or delicate pieces. But, as the definition of "cupboard" changed, it was given a broader meaning, to where it began to be used as a pantry or closet, as the intent and purpose changed. The purpose of a cupboard as it relates to a pantry is to store items deemed either perishable or non-perishable. In many cases, when items are deemed as "perishable," they have an expiration date or a "best if used by" marking. Items marked as "non-perishable" are thought not to have an expiration date, and usually can be used when needed. The purpose of cupboard as it relates to a closet is to store or put away things that one might not wear or display on a daily basis, such as suits, ties, shirts, hats, or dress shoes. Keep in mind. however, that closets and pantries aren't just for physical garments or consumable goods.

What Should Be in Your Cupboard?

Every "cupboard" is filled and stocked, not only to taste, but according to needs and environment. In my house, growing up as a child, and even as a parent, my cupboards went through "seasonal" changes, or re-stockings. These re-stockings were based on what season it was, and what was necessary for that season. For example, in the winter and fall months in my parents' pantry, I always remember there being lots of heavier foods, or foods that, for lack of a better choice of words, "stuck to your ribs." These usually consisted of beans, potatoes, rice, and things like hot breakfast foods. But in the warmer and summer months, I recall there not being so many heavy foods at all on the shelves. Instead, there were lots of cans of tuna, snack foods like chips and popcorn, and more dry cereals and quick foods.

The same applied to our closets and drawers. In the fall and winter months, we had heavier clothes, like sweaters, boots, and clothing more suitable to cooler climates and conditions. However, around spring break, we would do our annual spring cleaning, and we would put away all of our winter clothes and replace them with spring and summer clothes. Usually, we didn't have as many "summer clothes" as we did winter attire, because the months are shorter, and there wasn't a need to have on as much, because most of our time was spent playing and relaxing. I used that particular scenario to show the overall purpose of a cupboard or closet. They are for storing things that don't necessarily need to be on display all the time but are accessible when and if you need them. Most importantly, they are available to help you.

Taking Inventory of Your Cupboard

It is usually a daunting task to fill your cupboard or closet, because no one truly knows what they'll need. It's usually predicated upon your past experiences and endeavors, as well as the situations and circumstances that you've found yourself in. Honestly, no one can predict what life will bring. But, if you are mindful of your past and the things that you have encountered, then you will have a better gauge on how and what to store in your cupboard/closet, and if something out of the ordinary should arise, then you can make attempts to obtain the things to get you through that season, and store them for your next season, because they are bound to repeat themselves. An old axiom comes to mind concerning this, and that is something that Benjamin Franklin said: "An ounce of prevention is worth a pound of cure."

It has been my experience that it is easier to understand what you'll need for future endeavors based on past experiences, as opposed to what you already have. When you have been through something, and you didn't have the necessary tools or resources to perform your task, then it is easy to determine what you were lacking if you are wise, and wisdom is learned behavior based on failed experiences.

How to Fill Your Cupboard

First of all, let me make this perfectly clear: the filling of your cupboard should be about what is best for others, first, and then address what will benefit you. Remember, a true king's first allegiance is to your kingdom, and to making sure that your subjects are taken care of. The needs of the king should be secondary to the needs of his people. Therefore, when filling his cupboard, a true king looks at what will serve not only him, but his people.

There is a word that I came across unintentionally, and I found it while trying to help someone else with their initiative. I was looking up the word "incorruptible," and being one who likes to find out the more complete meaning of words, I looked at it in the Greek context and decided that a better word was "incorruptibility." The word that I found was "Aphtharsia," and its meaning is incorruptibility, indestructability, and immortality. This should be every king's goal, and that is the mark and distinction of being incorruptible. Every dream, aspiration, hope, and any other possession or ascension should be secondary.

I don't want to misconstrue the most important aspect concerning the filling of your cupboard, and that is that all that you seek to fill your cupboard with must be ordained, approved, and sanctioned by God. This is supported in both the Old and New Testaments, and also in every swearing in and instillation of kings: the help, sovereignty, and guidance of God is acknowledged and sought in the vow of fulfillment of duty. Psalm 127:1 says, "*Unless the Lord builds the house, those who build it labor in vain*" (ESV) What that means is, if God doesn't give you the plan, material, and know-how to fill your cupboard, then essentially, you are lost and will fill it amiss.

In Proverbs 21:1, it states: *"The king's heart is in the hand of the Lord, like the rivers of water; He turns it wherever He wishes."* (NKJV). Any and every good king, leader, or anyone who has authority should always, and in every situation, seek the heart, mind, and will of God, even in the seemingly most minute of decisions, because even those can have a great consequence concerning those he has rule over. So, it is even more painstakingly important that one who desires to be a king should dutifully and soberly consult God's Word, wisdom, and direction in the filling of his cupboard.

1. What Are Your Perishables?

The word "perishable" has several different meanings. Webster's Dictionary defines it as: "likely to spoil or decay; not likely to stay fresh for a long time if not eaten or used." The Greek word for "perishable" is "Phtartos," which means destruction, corruptible, or able to decay. Of course, there are things that we need in life, and in order to live, we must have material things. However, one must make sure while filling their cupboards that they don't just fill them with perishables. I have learned, and it has been proven, that perishable items have short shelf lives, and like all perishable goods, they are only good for a short time or season. Understand this: not only do food and consumable products expire, but clothes, cars, jewelry pieces, shoes, and just about everything you can put your hands on will eventually go out of style. Even credit cards have an expiration date, as do debit cards. It doesn't mean that your money runs out, but it does mean that you have to use something new to gain access to it.

Perishable items have their place in the world, but don't build your life around them, because in the end, even we are perishable. The most important things that you can have in your cupboard are things that give legacy and heritage, because every great king throughout history has been measured not solely by what his rule was, but also by what legacy remained after his reign. I admonish you not to be like the man who tore down his barns, after he saw how much he had acquired, and built new ones, and upon filling the new barns, he said to himself, "Soul, take thy rest." However, that very night, his soul was required of him by God. Never get so focused on your things that you stop pursuing the intangibles, like making sure that your life affects someone else's positively, for it is when your focus is there that your cupboard is truly full.

2. What Are Your Non-Perishables?

Non-perishable items are things that don't spoil, corrupt, decay, or go out of style. Simply put, non-perishables are good in any and every season, and effective in any situation. Earlier, I made mention of the Greek word "Aphtharsia," which means incorruptibility, indestructibility, and immortality. This one word is the foundation of what *The King's Cupboard* is and shall forever be built upon. In the previous segment, it was stated that a king's reign is measured by the legacy and heritage he leaves behind. Well, if Aphtharsia is the tenet he builds and fills his cupboard with, then all can rest assured that his will be a lasting legacy of honor.

Colossians 3:2 says, "*Set your affection on things above, not on things on the earth*" (KJV). In the pursuit of filling your cupboard, you must always ask the question, "God, do I need this?" If that answer is yes, then the second question should be "Why?" The key to filling your cupboard with non-perishable goods is to find the shopping list, and that list can only be found in the Word of God.

There are key items that should be in your cupboard, regardless of whether you are a godly person or not. If you are a person of good character, then the first thing on your list should be integrity.

Integrity means, according to the Oxford Dictionary :

1. The quality of being honest and having strong moral principles; moral uprightness.

2. The state of being whole and undivided.

This second definition stands out to me more than the first, because it brings to mind the scripture James 1:8, "*A double minded man is unstable in all his ways*" (KJV). It is impossible to rule or make wise decisions if you are in a state of instability or flux.

King Solomon was the wisest and wealthiest king in the history of the world. Some say that it was because of his wisdom that he accumulated great wealth and a great kingdom, but I beg to differ. I believe it was because of integrity that Solomon had great wealth and a great kingdom. The reason that I say this is that when Solomon was presented with the choice of having great riches or the ability to judge his people righteously, he chose the latter. This choice was simply the integrity to be upright and deal with God's people honorably, and because of this, God gave him not only great wisdom, but great wealth as well. When you take a stand to have integrity, there is nothing that God will withhold from you, because He knows that He can trust you. It says it in His Word. Psalm 84:11 says: "*For the Lord God is a sun and shield; the Lord bestows grace and favor and honor; no good thing will He withhold from those who walk uprightly*" (AMP).

This is why integrity is the first "non-perishable" that you should place in your cupboard, because whether you know it or not, God's first concern is His people and the treatment of them, and He desires a man who will put their needs before his own. If you are that kind of man, then great will be the days of your reign. It has become very evident to me that the first chapter of James is actually a very good template for the initial filling of your cupboard, concerning your "non-perishables." In James 1:3-4, the scriptures read: "*Knowing this, that the trying of your faith works patience. But let patience have her perfect work, that you may be perfect and entire, lacking in nothing*" (KJV2000). So, the next "non-perishable" is... yep, you guessed it: patience.

Patience is the most important attribute a leader can possess. That's because patience is not only about enduring, but it's about acquisition and possession. Luke 21:19 says: "*In your patience possess ye your souls*" (KJV). The ability to wait on God is very significant, because "wait on" can have two totally separate meanings, but they both require patience. Waiting as it relates to endurance and standing still is paramount when it comes to patience, because it says that you can be still until you get instructions on what's next. Waiting as it relates to serving God is still an exercise in patience, because in moving and serving, we sometimes move too fast and go before we are sent. Benjamin Franklin coined the phrase, "Haste makes waste." God honors the attribute of patience, because He knows that you have the character to handle anything that He gives you rule over. He also loves waiting as it relates to serving, because it is of the utmost importance to God. Jesus spoke several times about the importance of being a servant, because it takes patience to walk in servitude, and the result is promotion, not only spiritually, but in the world as well.

Jesus said, "*Whoever desires to be great among you, let him be your servant*" (Matthew 20:26, NKJV). If you have patience, then everything that God wants to do in you, with you, for you, and through you will come to pass. Patience allows you to access the needs of your people and make sure that they're addressed. Most importantly, patience will never let you supersede the will of God for your life, as some have done and ended up in calamity. Always remember that patience is the pacesetter in the race that keeps you from getting ahead of God and His plan.

Wisdom, as it is defined in Webster's Dictionary, is "the quality of having experience, knowledge, and good judgment; the quality of being wise." However, my own definition of wisdom is: knowledge gained from failed endeavors that says "don't do that again," or "don't make the same mistake." Again, the first chapter of James lends its unparalleled advice as to another "non-perishable" that should be stocked in your cupboard. James 1:5 says: "*If any of you lacks wisdom, let him ask of God, who gives to all men liberally, and reproaches not; and it shall be given him*" (KJV2000). Proverbs 4:7 (KJV) states:

"Wisdom is the principal thing; therefore, get wisdom: and with all thy getting get understanding" (KJV).

Both of these scriptures emphasize the importance of wisdom. The fourth chapter of Proverbs details how important it is to make wisdom a key commodity. Not everyone is blessed with wisdom, but everyone does have access to wisdom. God assures this in His Word. Further in this section, I will disclose how wisdom can be disseminated and obtained.

Wisdom is the key to any successful ruler's or leader's rule, and if wisdom is absent, then leadership is reckless, and the people will suffer. But, as important as wisdom is, without this next "non-perishable" item, and I dare say the most important in one's cupboard, all the other "non-perishables" will be unresolved and without aim and likened to shooting at a target with a shotgun, because this "non-perishable" gives all of the others focus and direction. That item is love.

Love has many definitions, and many have credibility, as they speak from an emotional or sexual connotation. The first definition (according to the Oxford Dictionary) reads: "an intense feeling of deep affection." The fourth definition says: "affectionate greetings conveyed to someone on one's behalf." Those are great; however, my definition, and the one that I think that God likes best, is: "A selfless act or gesture shown to another, where nothing but that person's or people's best interest is the only incentive."

You see, if you have all the other cupboard items, and don't have love, then none of the other "non-perishables" actually achieve their goal. In 1 Corinthians 13:1-2, the apostle Paul says:

> "If I speak in the tongues of men or of angels, but do not have love, I am only a resounding gong or a clanging cymbal. If I have the gift of prophesy and can fathom all mysteries and all knowledge, and if I have a faith that can move mountains, but do not have Love, I gain nothing." (NIV)

You see, love is the engine that makes the vehicle run. If you go down to verses 4 through 8 of the same chapter, they give clarity as to what love is, and what love is not. They read:

> "Love is patient, love is kind. It does not envy, it does not boast, it is not proud. It does not dishonor others, it is not self-seeking, it is not easily angered, it keeps no record of wrongs. Love does not delight in evil but rejoices with the truth. It always protects, always trusts, always hopes, always perseveres. Love never fails. But where there are prophecies, they will cease; where there are tongues, they will be stilled; where there is knowledge, it will pass away."

It goes on to say some more things, and they are significant, but in the conclusion of verse 13 it states, "But the greatest of these is love." If you noticed, every other "non-perishable" was basically addressed in the determining of what love is. So, I venture that it is safe, and even needful, to say that without love, none of the other items can truly exist, nor accomplish their goals.

It is my assessment that love and every other "non-perishable" item found in your cupboard are tools for servitude, and are placed in the cupboard (as it was stated in the beginning) to see how you as a king can serve others. Jesus said that all the commandments essentially come down to the first two: love God with all your heart and love your neighbor like you love yourself. If you keep these two things in your heart, mind, and cupboard, then you will never be led amiss.

3. What Are Your Must-Haves and Survival Necessities?

When it comes to must-haves and survival necessities, it is no secret that throughout history, great rulers, be they pagan or Christian, have sought out their false gods, or God Himself, whether it was for decisions to go to war, for peace, or simply how to rule over their people. This spoke to me in a very profound way, in that, if a ruler had enough understanding to seek guidance from a pagan deity that had no voice, or was not the true and living God, it clearly communicates that every ruler should seek the guidance of God in his everyday decisions. Well, God has made Himself available to us through His Word, His voice, and His presence. Therefore, the first must-have is a relationship with God. Is it safe to say that it is impossible to know the mind of a complete stranger? Well, the only way that you can know God is through relationship with Him, and I'm not talking about a passing prayer or a fleeting "Our Father." So, I tell you that the only way that you can truly know God's plans, and have relationship with Him, is through worship. I'm not talking Sunday morning worship service, either. It's hard to hear God's individual instruction in a corporate setting. No, I mean in His face, bow your knees, and yield your heart worship, because it is there and only there that you can hear the expressed, clear, and concise voice of God. So, this is a survival necessity, and a "must-have" for your cupboard.

Some may think that I'm "putting the cart before the horse" in this, but the next "must-have" is the Word of God. I put these in this order, because one can know the Word of God backward and forward, but if it is just scripture, then it will never come alive, nor give life. John 1:1 says:

> "In the beginning was the Word, and the Word was with God, and the Word was God."

Now, if God and His Word are the same, then it would (at least in my estimation) behoove a person to know God first, because if you know God, then you know that He only speaks through His Word, but the physical Word of God tells us His promises and acts as a "Living Will and Last Testament" that speaks to all that one can expect and look forward to, and it also fills in the blanks in the parts that we miss. Every king establishes the laws of his kingdom by decree. Well, the Word of God is His ironclad, undeniable, and binding decree.

I saved this "must-have" for last, because many will not attain this level, and though they may become great rulers over whatever kingdom God may give them, they will not be the very best that they can be. The "must-have" or "survival necessity" that I'm referring to is the heart of God. Having or knowing the heart of God can only be obtained one way, and most people aren't willing to sacrifice themselves enough to gain it: it is by becoming a "Friend of God." There have only been a handful of men who have attained the title or earned the distinction of being God's friend, and they were Enoch, Abraham, Moses, Job, David, Daniel, Isaiah, and I believe the apostle Paul.

The term "Friend of God" is the highest privilege and honor one can have bestowed upon them, because if God calls you friend, then everything that is on the heart of God for His people, He reveals to His friend. "Friends of God" are few and far between, because only a few men in the history of the world have been given that distinction, and it didn't come because of great power, wealth, or conquest. No, it was achieved through the most difficult battle that we can fight, self-surrender and yieldedness. Look at the lives and stories of each of these men, and aside from Enoch, God used each of them to write the most powerful books of the Bible. It just further corroborates my statement that if you want to know God's plan for His people, then you must walk with Him.

The Ascension to Kingship

Every boy is born with the ability to be a king inside of him. The sad truth is, most boys grow into adult men and never have this innate regality nurtured. There are countless men who have greatness within them but were born to fathers who had peasant mindsets. The truth, especially in the Kingdom of God, is that we were given the right to be heirs to the kingdom through the spirit of adoption. What most people don't understand about adoption is that the adopted child actually has more legal rights than a naturally born child.

Also, there are many scriptures that give credence to God foreknowing us before we were born and having a plan for our lives. However, there is one legacy to royalty in 1 Peter 2:9, which states:

> *"But ye are a chosen generation, a royal priesthood, a holy nation, a peculiar people; that ye should shew forth the praises of him who hath called you out of darkness into his marvelous light."* (KJV)

This scripture doesn't just say that we are able to be kings and priests, it declares and mandates that it is our responsibility to be so.

The Mark Twain classic, *The Prince and the Pauper* tells of a poor boy of low estate who wanders too close to the palace wall and sees the prince, the future King of England. Being identical in appearance, they decide to switch places and live each other's lives. In actuality, this has already taken place, because Christ has already switched places with us, so that we can live in royalty and be seated on the throne. 1 John 3:2 says:

> *"Beloved, now are we the sons of God, and it doth not yet appear what we shall be: but we know that, when he shall appear, we shall be like him; for we shall see him as he is."* (KJV)

Ascension to kingship isn't about whether you were born into royalty, because God made provision through Christ that once we accept Him, we are engrafted into the kingdom. No, the ascension isn't physical, and although we are blood transfused, the ascension is realizing that you have the right, both legally and spiritually, to rule in whatever territory God gives you, because now we are His sons!

It is the aim and design of *The King's Cupboard* to unlock and unleash the king that is inside of every man, and to teach them, so that they can train boys to recognize and realize their potential through servitude and surrender.

1. Foundational Necessities

No king starts off as a king. Although he will be king one day, he must first understand that he is a prince, and he has set guidelines that he must subject himself to and protocols that he must follow. Although a prince is an heir to the throne, he is taught that he has rules that he must adhere to. Also, he is given over to tutors that he is subject to, and he is taught by them, and they give reports of his progress to the king. Although a prince has some authority, he does not have full authority. Thus, he does not have the ability to make decrees and declarations. A prince has to ask permission of those over him to do the smallest of things. This is done to remind him that there is always a higher authority that he must answer to. A king who doesn't understand that he answers to an ultimate authority will become reckless and ruthless, and in most cases, such kings will be removed from the throne, usually by the very people he has rule over.

It is always necessary for every living thing to be nursed, then crawl, then walk, and ultimately run. If this process isn't followed, then the bones (foundation) don't become strong enough, and at first falling, there is sure to be a break sustained. It's good to crawl before you walk, because crawling teaches humility.

I'm reminded of a story that my parents told me; they say it occurred when I was a baby. Apparently, I learned how to walk relatively early in my development. We lived on the third floor of an apartment building. After falling down the stairs on my first attempt to navigate them, I learned to make my way down slowly, one stair at a time. One particular day, I was feeling myself, and I decided to go all the way down to the first floor. Well, needless to say, I didn't have the strength nor the know-how to get back up, and someone had to come down and get me. If the foundation isn't made strong, then someone will always have to come down and get you, due to your decisions.

2. Growth Acknowledgments

I think back to when I was a smaller child, and in our bedroom closet, there were four names with lines drawn in pencil and pen beneath them. These names were of my two older brothers, me, and my then-youngest brother. Every few months, my dad would take his tape measure and a level, and then mark off how tall we were and how much each of us had grown. It was fun for a while, and it was especially fun when I had grown more than my brothers, but it was disappointing when I learned that I hadn't grown that much.

After my two youngest brothers were born, my dad didn't measure us anymore, and the only way that I could tell that I had grown was that my clothes got smaller, or should I say, that they didn't fit anymore. Also, my shoes got tighter, and I started to catch up to my mother and surpass her in height.

Just like my dad measured us, life and experiences have a way of doing the same thing. The thing is, unlike Dad, life won't mark off your growth. You only learn that you are growing because you experience growing pains, or certain things just don't fit any longer. As a king, you don't know you have grown until a problem, uprising, or some form of rebellion occurs, and you don't handle it the same way you once did. As a matter of fact, you don't even view it the same way. You see, a kingly or regal perspective always looks at things from an elevated view. As a king, you don't look at things or situations from a subject's point of view. No, everything is looked at from a solution orientation, and not a problem-based one. The mind of a king is achieved when pettiness is removed from your thoughts, and how you once looked at a problem isn't how you address it now.

A wise ruler doesn't perceive problems emotionally. He looks at them in terms of "How will this affect my kingdom?" If you don't look at life from a "what is best for subjects" standpoint, and you still make reactionary decisions as opposed to proactive responses or initiatives, then you are not fit to rule, and you have more growing to do. But if you act as a king, that is, not swayed by emotion or triggered by your feelings, then you can acknowledge your growth and rest assured that you and your kingdom will be enlarged.

3. Understanding Where You Are Deficient

According to the Oxford Dictionary, "deficient" means "not having enough of a specified quality or ingredient." Everyone is deficient or has a deficiency in one area or another. Some people don't have enough patience, while some don't have enough knowledge, and some don't have enough love, etc. The key to becoming whole in your deficiency is not to focus on the areas where you are deficient, but to be honest with yourself concerning them. You have to acknowledge your deficiencies, as many of us have more than one. It takes courage to lead, and to lead effectively, it takes courage and character. It takes both to admit to oneself that "I'm lacking," or simply "I'm not good enough" in the area where you are deficient. It takes honesty and a pure heart to admit when we "don't cut the mustard," because as human beings, we all like to think that we have it all together. However, 2 Peter 1:3-8 tells us:

> "According as his divine power hath given unto us all things that pertain unto life and godliness, through the knowledge of him that hath called us to glory and virtue: Whereby are given to us exceeding great and precious promises: that by these ye might be partakers of the divine nature, having escaped the corruption that is in the world through lust. And beside this, giving all diligence, add to your faith virtue; and to virtue knowledge; and to knowledge temperance; and to temperance patience; and to patience godliness; and to godliness brotherly kindness; and to brotherly kindness charity. For if these things be in you, and abound, they make you that ye shall neither be barren nor unfruitful in the knowledge of our Lord Jesus Christ." (KJV)

Yes, it is very difficult to admit that we have deficiencies. But, if we are to be good rulers over the kingdom God gives us, then we have to have an earnest desire within ourselves to be all that we can be, not just for our own sake, but for the sake of those we lead and have rule over. It takes passion to want to see people be their best, but it takes strength of heart to acknowledge deficiencies, and to turn your weakness into strengths.

Deficiencies are only bad when you allow the spirit of self-righteousness to keep you from changing. I was once told, "It's okay to be wrong, but it's never okay to stay wrong."

Chapter II

Courage

The Man Who Would Be King

As I stated earlier, it is a monumental task to acknowledge that we are deficient in an area or, God forbid, more than one. However, it takes a phenomenal amount of courage to even attempt to lead, and to be responsible for others and their well-being. But can you imagine the intestinal fortitude it must take to access something within you that you have never been, or aren't sure if you are even capable of being? For the man who would be king, there has to be a tremendous amount of fear to overcome, at least if he's human and cares about the well-being of others. Any leader who has never been the "Big Boss" has to feel tremendous anxiety when challenged with the task of being the one who sets the policies, makes the rules, hands out the discipline, and ultimately is responsible for whether the ship sails or sinks.

I've held leadership positions in the business sector, the church community, and the athletic world, and in all those job titles, one question always arose in my mind. Even as a husband and father, that question would arise, and that question was,

"Am I good enough to do this?" If you care about people, then you'd better ask yourself that question, and finding out if you are is on-the-job training.

This is what you should understand as you are in training, and accessing your kingly qualities, while you wait for your kingdom. Romans 13:1 says, "*Let every soul be subject unto the higher powers. For there is no power but of God.*" (KJV). The powers that be are ordained of God. So, if God has called you to be king over anything, or anyone, then He has ordained you to be so. However, understand this. If you desire to be a ruler, know that you will make some mistakes, and every now and then, you will "blow it." But if God places you as head over anything, then always lead as if it is a privilege and not a right, because that will determine your length of rule.

1. What Are Kingly Requirements?

The list of requirements for kingship isn't necessarily long, but it runs very deep, and it will test your mettle. Luke 12:48 says, "*For unto whomsoever much is given, of him shall be much required.*" (KJV). The first requirement on the list has to be an exaggerated degree of selflessness. This characteristic is vitally necessary because it is the chief cornerstone and foundation that every truly great kingdom is built upon. The greatest kingdom known to man is the kingdom of heaven; both God and Christ had to make huge sacrifices of selflessness in order to redeem man. God's was the sacrifice of yielding His Son, and Christ's was yielding His life for us, and doing so to something that he had no concept of, the commission of sin.

Selflessness always puts the mission before the well-being of the missionary. It is always expected of the soldier that he/

she may lose their life in battle, but they take on the possibility of such sacrifice so that the war can be won. Every great king, leader, or even family patriarch should have a selflessness within him that supersedes his own benefit and instead looks forward to what will benefit his kingdom. John F. Kennedy said these words in his inauguration speech in 1961: "Ask not what your country can do for you; ask what you can do for your country." This should be the mantra of every man who would be king.

Next there has to be an enormous hunger for righteousness. Previously, you read the word "Aphtharsia"; again, this is a Greek word that means incorruptibility, indestructibility, and immortality. This word is paramount, because it is, or should be, the foundation for every decision that a leader makes. If God's righteousness is not the goal for every plan, and ultimately the outcome of those plans, then your plans will fail. In the Gospel according to Matthew, Jesus asked his disciples, "*Whom do men say that I the Son of man am?*" After many gave their different answers, Jesus asked Peter, who declared, "*Thou art the Christ, the Son of the living God.*" Jesus replied, "*Blessed art thou, Simon Bar-Jonah: for flesh and blood hath not revealed it unto thee, but my Father which is in heaven. And I say also unto thee, that thou art Peter, and upon this rock I will build my church; and the gates of hell shall not prevail against it*" (Matthew 16:13-18, KJV). You see, righteousness is another name for God's truth, and if you make your decisions in it, then they will always stand and be well founded, because righteousness will never die, nor can it be corrupted.

In the process of becoming a king, there are many lessons and characteristics that you will have to learn over and over again, because they have to become a part of who and what you are. I was told, "You have to do something at least one thousand times before it becomes a habit." Well, good attributes don't become a habit if you only do them once. Forgive me, because I omitted a word in my quote, and that word is "consistently." Good and bad habits become habits through consistency. Righteousness, selflessness, courage, and love have to be practiced consistently in order for them to become pillars of character, much like lying, stealing, killing, drinking, smoking, womanizing, etc., have to be practiced, to form bad character traits.

Courage isn't necessary just to fight battles. No, it is necessary to fight battles within, and even to make hard decisions, and to do the things that you don't want to do, for the good of your kingdom or for the benefit of your people. Courage, or the pursuit of it, will cause you many sleepless nights, because courage is not making the popular decision. No, courage in most cases is making the decision that no one likes or understands, and courage is a heavy burden to bear. That's why it is said, "Heavy is the head that wears the crown." One who makes a decision to address and access the king that they desire to be must do so vigilantly and soberly, if they desire to be the best king they can be.

Last, but certainly not least – and yes, you have seen this word before as well – is love. I cannot reiterate enough how important it is to have love in every action, decision, and thought that you make for and towards your people, because another word for love is charity or benevolence, and anything you do from a charitable or benevolent aspect is done with the benefit of others in mind. Love is an attribute that will never serve you in the wrong way, or even let you be taken advantage of, even if the intention of another is to do so. The three forms that won't allow you to be taken advantage of are Agape, Philia, and Pragma. Agape is the love that God has for us, and it is based in an unselfish love, or a form of altruism. Its whole purpose is predicated upon the foundation of love for the benefit of others. Philia is a friendly love, or "brotherly love," and is based upon the tenets of good will and virtue. The last is Pragma, and that love is based on duty and the long-term interest of others.

There are actually four other types of Love, but they are based on emotion and condition, and they really can't be applied here, because they are subject to change based on the actions of others. The three forms of love named here are for the benefit of others and have no ulterior motives, because they are not self-serving, neither do they attempt to gain anything in return for doing "the right thing." Even if the people you are sacrificing for are contrary, unappreciative, and manipulative in nature, it's okay, because you are giving and showing love for love's sake. 1 Peter 4:8 says, "*Above all, love each other deeply, because love covers over a multitude of sins.*" (NIV). So, love even when you are not the sinner.

2. About Your Consorts

Your consort, by definition, is extremely pertinent, because the word itself means "the wife, husband, or companion of a reigning monarch." Consorts are very important because they have great influence over and with leaders and the decisions they make. So, it is vitally important that a person who is consort to a king be one of great wisdom and sound judgment.

There is an old axiom that says, "Show me your company, and I'll tell you who you are." There is also one that says, "Birds of a feather flock together." These are both proven quotes, to the good and the bad. However, I shall use my own quote to the bad, and a scripture to the good. The quote is, "One who is the constant company of the foolish will himself become a fool." Now, the scripture that I would use is Proverbs 11:14: "*Where there is no counsel, the people fall; but in the multitude of counselors there is safety*" (KJV). It is very unwise to make decisions alone, but it is catastrophic to make decisions by the advice of the unwise.

The worst thing any king or leader can do is surround themselves with "yes men," because no good ever comes from a person who is a "brown-nose." King Solomon, who was the wisest king in history, wrote the wisdom encyclopedia known today as Proverbs. In that book, he poured out quotes that were full of wisdom, life guidance, and direction. One such quote is Proverbs 27:6, which reads: "*Wounds from a friend can be trusted, but an enemy multiplies kisses*" (NIV). Simply put, a friend will tell you the truth, even if it hurts you, but an enemy will tell you what you want to hear, only to gain favor.

A good king always should want good counsel around them and make every attempt to weed out those who would give bad counsel, even if it is a spouse, sibling, or parent. Although we hate to think this way, sometimes those closest to us don't have our best interests at heart. Make sure that you do this one thing for certain, found in 1 Thessalonians 5:12: "*And we beseech you, brethren, to know them which labor among you, and are over you in the Lord, and admonish you*" (KJV). I have had people who were very close to me offer me some very poor advice. Was it done to hurt me in the long run? I don't know. Or was it based on bad training and upbringing that they had received? It doesn't matter, because ultimately, the information and advice that they gave me was reckless to my life. Don't ever allow people that have cracks in their walls help you lay the foundation to build your house.

3. Your Mentors and Trainers

Every king or leader, and even a man who desires to be a husband and father someday, should have a mentor or a guide. This process should never stop, because we all are always growing and obtaining knowledge, wisdom, and understanding, and we should desire to do so up until the day we die. Every boy is a prince, even if the father is the worst of kings and has the most pitiful of kingdoms. If that is the case, then he too will grow to be a worthless monarch. However, if he is fortunate, a man who is wise, kingly, and knowledgeable will see his dilemma, take him under his wing, and tutor him in the ways of growing into wearing the crown.

In past times and even today, princes were raised by mentors and had trainers. In most cases, the prince spent more time with his mentor than he did with his own father, the king. He only spent time with the king when the king was holding court or having social interaction. It is very disheartening to me that this practice of kings letting mentors raise their heirs is still done today, but we'll address that later.

A wise king understands that he is king until he dies, is removed by revolt, or abdicates his throne. The wisest of kings understands that he needs mentors and training for every step, decision, and proclamation of his kingship, and he will never stop having the need to get wisdom and to gain insight. Even when one of those mentors passes, the king should always seek out one who he feels is wiser than himself, because the reason that a mentor exists is to give substance, solidify. or give resolve to thoughts and actions. The suffix "-ment" itself means "to give concrete result to an action, object, or process." A wise man once said, "No man is an island, no man stands alone." Every great king built his kingdom on the shoulders of those who held him up, and so should you.

4. How to Enter and Exit

Knowing how to enter and exit before God's people, or the people you lead, is an extremely important skill to master, and quite a necessary one, if you desire to gain and maintain the trust and respect of those you have rule over.

In 2 Chronicles 1:10, King Solomon was asked by God what he wanted God to give him, and Solomon answered, "*Give me now wisdom and knowledge, that I may go out and come in before this people: for who can judge this thy people, that is so great?*" (KJV). Solomon understood the humility of servitude, even as a king. You see, a wise king enters and exits the same way, and that is in the shroud of grace and humility, because both these attributes can be trusted. A leader, be it a king, president, CEO, or pastor, should be announced. However, in most cases, if he has the heart and pulse of the people, and they his then they will always watch in waiting for his appearance, and a grand exclamation won't be necessary.

Entering a situation as a king should be done in the humblest of manners. The graciousness of a king's entrance gives his people the comfort that he is there to serve them in the capacity of one privileged to be in their midst, and not they in his. If this is the procedure, then that king along with his sound judgement will always have the confidence of the people. As wise and as honorable as Solomon was when he started his reign, toward the end of it, he became a foolish king, and that's because he didn't keep God as the focus of his affection. Any king that does not rely on the providence of God as his leading will always exit in shame.

I'm reminded of my leader, as it relates to how he enters and exits the sanctuary. In most cases, many people don't know when he comes in. He leaves only after speaking a blessing over the people, but he never comes in with any pomp and circumstance, because he comes in with one thought, and that is to serve God and His people. It is never about him, and as a leader, it should never be about you, or about you receiving any glory. No, entering and exiting should be done inconspicuously, because kingship is not about a show or spotlights. It's about the One who brought us out of darkness and into His marvelous light.

5. How to Adorn Yourself with Kingly Apparel

No matter how flashy a king's clothes are, or how many jewels may encrust his crown, or how beautiful his lion's head is over his cloak – that's a reference to the movie *Coming to America*, if you haven't seen it – the symbols that make him king, or are the signs of his authority, are his crown, his scepter, and his robe or mantle. Everything else is just for show. When Saul was first made King of Israel, his crown wasn't haughty. Actually, it was rather common and plain. His scepter wasn't gaudy or splendid, nor was his robe. Quite frankly, all of his adornment was rudimentary and basic. When we want to glorify the objects that represent our kingship, it is then that we lose the ability to wear them correctly.

The head that wears the crown should be one that is capable of staying straight and being held steady, because the weight of most crowns is very heavy, and the more jewels you have placed in it, the heavier it becomes. Actually, it is your neck that supports the weight of the crown, and the neck is related to your support system. I guarantee that if your neck is not strong, then your entire body will suffer deformities, experience great pain, and make it difficult to stand, and so shall it be for your kingdom. If your neck does not rest on strong shoulders, then the weight of the crown will become unbearable, and as opposed to being an honor to wear, it will become more like a curse.

The next thing is your robe, or mantle. The mantle is representative of the anointing and authority of the office that God has ordained for you (or ordained you for). The one thing about a robe or mantle is that if it's too loose, you can't wear it or keep it on, and if it's too small, then you'll end up tearing it or splitting it at its seams. It is important to have a mantle that was blessed by God, but made for you, because you cannot fit another king's anointing. As beautiful as other people's garments may be, in kingship, there is no such thing as "one size fits all." No, they are tailor made to God's specifications to fit you, and you, alone.

How many of you remember dressing up in your parents' clothes when you were little? As fun as it may have been, and as grown up as you may have felt, when you looked in the mirror, you looked ridiculous. That's how you look to God, and to other people, when you try and wear someone else's mantle. Make sure that it's made to fit your shoulders, or it will fall off. When Saul tried to dress David in his armor, David said, "I can't wear this, it's too big. Plus, I haven't proven this." David was wise enough to understand what he was anointed to use, and it worked, because he had proven experience with it.

The same principle applies to a ruler's scepter. A scepter is a symbol of power, and it can often be used for a king to lean on. Yes, it is sometimes necessary for a king to rest, and there is absolutely nothing wrong with a king resting on the power and authority that God has given him, because the power is God, and He requires us to rest in His power.

A scepter is much like the weapon of a police officer. It is his ultimate symbol of power, but the thing is, most police officers don't use the exact same weapon. When a police department mandates a force to carry a particular modeled weapon, you can rest assured that there will be modifications made to the grip, the barrel, or the butt, because that weapon is ultimately that officer's power, and they have to be in control of it and the decisions that cause them to wield its power.

In adorning kingly apparel, understand that you must make sure that you identify your specifications, because either way... they don't change.

Fighting Your Dragons

Every kingdom has enemies, or adversaries. I like to call them dragons. Your dragons are any person, place, or thing that comes to try and take over, destroy, or even prevent you from creating your kingdom. In order to have success as a king, you will have to fight your dragons. However, in building and protecting your kingdom, you must identify your dragons and devise a plan of battle to defeat them. In this section, I will help you discern, identify, and defeat your dragons.

1. Proper Posture

When going into battle or fighting any adversary, it is extremely important to have the appropriate posture. In just about every circumstance of battle, it is always reiterated that the low man wins. Whether it is actual combat, sports, or even cards, one is taught to stay low, or keep your hand where no one can see it. This is in large part because it is hard to hit what you can't see.

In all levels of strategic opposition, you never expose yourself to your enemy until he is defenseless against your attack, and it is only then that you unleash your full strength. I have been a football coach for over thirty years, and most of that time was spent coaching offensive and defensive linemen. The thing is it is very hard to train linemen to stay in the proper posture for successful achievement at their position. The reason is because it is natural to always want to be in an upright position, but in your natural upright posture, you possess very little power or strength. It is only when one diminishes himself to a smaller level that he will become strong enough for battle. As a result of this fact, I spent most of my time initially teaching my guys how to "stay low" and learn how to become comfortable in an uncomfortable position.

Eventually, my players found out that the lower they remained, the more success they had. They even developed an encouragement when they broke the huddle, and that was simply "stay low." There is nothing one can achieve in a position of pride, especially in battle or conflict, both naturally and spiritually.

The Word of God says in 1 Peter 5:6: "Humble yourselves therefore under the mighty hand of God, that he may exalt you in due time" (KJV).

It is in times of struggle and intense conflict that we should become more humble and not show how strong we are within ourselves. We should yield our nature to the will and guidance of God, and stay as small as possible, because if it's about us, then it will never be about Him. Goliath went about making threats against the Army of Israel and was very loud and visible doing so. However, in the end, it was a small, runty boy who took his life. It is in our weakness, or our humble state, that God's strength is made perfect. Always remember this: the taller the building, the wider the foundation has to be. Make sure that you are always big in your foundation (relationship with God), so when it is time to rise up, you have the strength and the support to stand.

2. Selecting Your Weapons of Warfare

Selecting your weapons of warfare is based on knowledge and wisdom, especially about what you are fighting against and what your circumstances are. If I am trying to battle a grease fire, then I definitely don't want to throw water on it. No, I want to use salt, or cover it with a lid. Just like you don't use a mouse trap to catch a fly, understanding the weapons of your warfare is as important as understanding the enemy you are fighting.

I remember in the movie *Ghostbusters*, the Ghostbusters couldn't fight spiritual entities with natural weapons, such as guns or knives. No, they had to use weapons of immense light to subdue and capture creatures of spiritual wickedness. Ephesians 6:11-13 says it best:

> "Put on the whole armor of God, that ye may be able to stand against the wiles of the devil. For we wrestle not against flesh and blood, but against principalities, against powers, against the rulers of the darkness of this world, against spiritual wickedness in high places. Wherefore take unto you the whole armor of God, that ye may be able to withstand in the evil day, and having done all, to stand." (KJV)

The armor of God is His Word, and if you equip yourself with that, then in every situation, you can and will be victorious. The Word will teach you what to use, and the greatest weapon is the Holy Spirit, because he has a 100 percent successful battle record, and he is an annihilator of wickedness. Remember, don't ever bring a knife to a gun fight, and never bring your flesh to a spiritual war.

3. Realization of Your Strengths and Weaknesses

Every king, ruler, or leader has strengths, because it takes strengths to ascend to a throne. However, it has been shown throughout history that every king has had weaknesses as well. Saul had them, David had them, Solomon had them, and so has every king and leader that has succeeded them and gone before them. It's called being human. No one born in this life has ever been born without weaknesses. Even the King of Kings had weaknesses that he had to address before he made his walk to Calvary's cross. The thing is, he embraced, recognized, and overcame all of those weaknesses with this one word, which is formed from three, and that word is "nevertheless."

According to the Oxford Dictionary, the word "nevertheless" means "in spite of that, notwithstanding, all the same." Regardless of the fact that weakness is present, the embracing of said weakness makes us victorious and causes triumph. Mind you, I didn't say succumbing to weakness, but embracing it. It is easy to recognize one's own strengths and how to grow stronger in them, and actually, you should. But understanding your weaknesses and seeking to make them strengths creates balance and makes a king hard to dethrone.

Overcoming your weakness takes determination, hard work, and patience. As it was stated earlier, "*Let patience have her perfect work, that ye may be perfect and entire, wanting nothing*" (James 1:4, KJV). "Perfect," as it is used in this scripture, doesn't mean without flaw. No, it means mature, and you should understand that weakness is a sign of immaturity. Whatever your strengths and weaknesses are, embrace them, but more importantly, recognize them, and don't pretend that they don't exist. Always stay before God and ask Him to be strong in your weakness.

A great place to start is the "Serenity Prayer." The word "serenity" itself denotes calmness, peacefulness, and being untroubled. As you start praying this prayer in earnest, and working toward being made perfect, you will find that it is okay to have weaknesses, but not to stay weak. The Serenity Prayer helps you in asking God to recognize and discern strengths and weaknesses, and to get understanding in knowing how to distinguish them. It reads:

> "Lord, grant me the serenity to accept the things I cannot change, courage to change the things that I can, and wisdom to know the difference."

Knowing how to recognize your strengths and weaknesses is paramount in becoming a good king. David was a great example of this: he was quick to acknowledge his weaknesses, and it made him the apple of God's eye. It didn't make him perfect, but it made his heart perfect, and a man like that, God can always use.

4. Strategy for Battle

When you are opposed by something or someone, or you are having conflict with an entity or group, then you have to create a strategy for battle. However, not all battles have to be bloody all-out wars. No, some battles are fought intellectually, some spiritually, and some legally, but whatever the battle is, there has to be intel gathered and a game plan devised. A game plan is just another name for a strategy for battle, whatever the battlefield. You have to understand what type of battle it is that you are fighting. Not every battle requires brute force. Some battles are won by finessing your opponent. Some battles are won by outthinking, and the battle of Jericho was won through endurance and obedience. Great leaders understand, better than their enemy, where their enemy is both strongest and weakest. Most great strategists use an enemy's strength against them and exploit that enemy's weakness.

The same goes for us in our spiritual battles. You can't fight a spiritual force through natural means. 2 Corinthians 10:4 says: *"For the weapons of our warfare are not of the flesh but have divine power to destroy strongholds"* (ESV).

However, the enemy would attack us naturally in our lives, by attacking our finances, our marriages, and our families. If the devil knows that you are fortified in your prayer, worship, fasting, and your offering life, then he won't try and attack you there. No, just ask Job : the devil is going to attack the thing most important to many of us, our children, and then our health.

The key to strategizing a battle plan is not just waging war but attacking the enemy where it hurts most. As I mentioned before, the devil attacks us where we hurt most, in our flesh and our feelings. Well, you can't fight the enemy physically, because he is not flesh and blood. So, instead of fighting him physically, you fight him spiritually. What is most important to the devil? Souls. You go out and you destroy his kingdom by snatching souls away from him, and you tear down his kingdom that way. I guarantee, if you fight your enemy where he is strongest, then you will lose. But if you make him weaker where he is weakest, then I assure you that he will concede and leave you alone.

Understanding Your Armor: What Armor Do You Require?

Understanding your armor is vitally important as it relates to battles and what type of wars you are waging, and what is being waged against you. Not all wars and battles are the same. Some are waged by small and sneaky adversaries, and some by forces of great size, strength, and magnitude. Some are natural and some spiritual. However, whatever battle you fight, the determining factors of how you fare are your battle strategies, reconnaissance, and, most crucially, what type of armor is appropriate for that particular battle.

The armor you require is solely determined by what enemy you are fighting and the conditions of the battle. For example, if I am waging war at sea, then it doesn't behoove me to try and use tanks to destroy my enemy. No, I would need boats, ships, submarines, and aircraft to fight that war. Another example is that if I am playing basketball, then I don't show up dressed in football equipment. You must understand who and what you are at war against in order to properly select your armor.

In the previous section, I addressed the strategy for battle. Battle strategy dictates whether a war will be won or lost. However, the armor you wear is just as important as your battle plan. Take the United States Armed Forces, for example. During different campaigns, our uniforms have changed based on battle conditions and environments. In tropical conditions, the issued uniform and tactical equipment was camouflage green, but in the Afghanistan conflict, the uniforms were sandy in color.

Different conditions require different modes of dress. It's funny how both firemen and police officers have the main objective of saving lives, yet a policeman would be ill-equipped to fight crime in firefighters' gear, just as a firefighter would appear foolish running into a burning building with a bulletproof vest and guns only and expecting to extinguish and survive a fire.

In the book of Ephesians 6:10-18, the apostle Paul speaks about the whole armor of God, and about putting it on so that you can stand in the evil day against the devil. It further goes into detail about what the "whole armor" consists of. It gives descriptions of the battle conditions and environment, but most importantly, it gives explicit detail about the armor, what it is, and what it should cover. Many people don't understand it, but everything that the armor covers is critical for you to protect in order to come out of battle alive, both naturally and spiritually. When you get an opportunity, read the passage in its entirety, and you will see that in whatever battle you fight, there is a need for some form of the armor pieces named. It names the armor that will protect your head/mind, chest/heart, loins/sexual purity and integrity, and a shield that protects you from all forms of character assassination attempts. It gives a sword that helps you fight and slay all forms of evil. And last but not least, it covers your feet, because without them, you cannot advance in battle or gain ground on the enemy. However, did you notice that it leaves no protection for your back? That's because if you are pressing and advancing in God's plan, then you never have to watch your back, because God has that covered.

1. Is Your Armor Adequate for Your Particular Battle?

It was mentioned in the previous section that armor has to be battle appropriate. Meaning, does your armor allow you the proper movement, balance, and vision necessary for battle? Some battles are fought with quicker, faster, and more agile foes. If that is the case, then you don't need big, bulky armor. No, you need armor that is light, flexible, and built for agility. I am reminded of the movie *Iron Man*: when Tony Stark first built his first unit, it was built for a short, quick battle, and it didn't need to go far or be very mobile. However, when he started building his next set of armor, and everyone after that, every set became stronger and more accessible, but could do more things and take more punishment. Your armor should be like Tony Stark's Mark VII armor. It is always accessible, because it was coded to his anatomy, and like its prototype, the Holy Spirit, it is always locked on to your signal, and always ready to cover you in battle, no matter where it may be.

2. Does Your Armor Fit You?

Armor should fit you the same way as any well-tailored suit. A poorly fitting suit, no matter how much it cost, or what accessories you try and dress it up with, is basically useless, for all practical purposes. Well, that's the same scenario as armor that doesn't fit you. It is very difficult to do battle in armor that's too small or too big. The main reason is that it does not give you the ability to move with freedom. Understand this: we aren't talking about physical armor, because, honestly speaking, who goes around wearing armor in this day and age? This armor is in the metaphorical sense. One's sets of spiritual and intellectual armor are the most important armor that you can possess, and if you have outgrown it, or simply haven't matured enough to fit the armor that the battle mandates, then how can you fight appropriately?

Spiritually, if you are involved in a battle, then you have to know how big you really are, and more important, how big the demon you are fighting is, and the stronghold it encompasses. You can't pretend that you are a size 54 athletic, when in actuality, you are a 38 regular, and being realistic about your size allows you to go to war where you're at. It reminds me of the nineteenth chapter of the book of Acts, when the seven sons of Sceva called themselves casting out demons in possessed people. They went to lay hands on one man, and he told them, "*Jesus I know, and Paul I recognize, but who are you?*" (Acts 19:15, ESV), and he proceeded to whip them out of their clothes.

If you don't fast, worship, or pray in the Holy Spirit, then how can you expect to wear XL armor when you are actually a size medium? Romans 12:3 says: "*Do not think of yourself more highly than you ought, but rather think of yourself with sober judgment, in accordance with the faith God has distributed to each of you*" (NIV).

It is okay to want to be bigger than you are, but realize where you are, and what size armor is appropriate to your faith. It's the same situation intellectually. If you have the understanding of a fifth grader, then trying to match wits with a college professor is foolish. It is your responsibility to grow and enlarge your capacity of thought and acumen. 2 Timothy 2:15 says: "*Study to show yourself approved unto God, a workman that needs not to be ashamed, rightly dividing the word of truth*" (KJV2000).

It is fine to have a desire to grow, and even to be better, but if you attempt to wear armor that you aren't suited for, then every battle you attempt to fight will end disastrously. Adequately fitting armor is your responsibility and owning where you are is your accountability as well. and If you don't take responsibility for your stake, then every battle you fight will be a losing one, because you can't navigate your armor.

Much like adequately battle-appropriate armor, it is very necessary to have armor that fits you. Simply put, does the armor that you want to wear fit you? It is very difficult to wear someone else's anointing. Have you ever tried to wear someone else's shoes after they have been broken in? I must tell you, it is a very awkward experience, and that's because shoes broken in by someone else have a different lean, heel wear, and stretching, so trying to wear someone else's shoes is very uncomfortable. What most don't understand about wearing another person's shoes is that it isn't that the shoe itself is deformed or out of shape. No, it's because they walk different, and how you walk wasn't created to match how they walk. The reason why is that God created each of us with a specific anointing, and a unique purpose and people we were created to reach. I am not exactly sure of what armor fits me, but I do know that I wasn't created to wear anyone else's. God is not so limited in His ability to create that He has to recycle someone else's armor and give it to you. There are not enough situations that can occur, or so many battles to fight, for you to have to wear someone else's armor. God has a suit of armor that is, was, and will be fitted for you, and as you grow, so will your armor. There is enough God to make a big enough suit of armor for little ole you.

3. Has Your Armor Been Fortified?

First, let's get straight to the point, so that we can understand what "fortified" means and make clear why it is so important to ensure that one's armor is fortified. The definition of fortify (according to Webster's Dictionary) is "to strengthen (a place) with defensive works, so as to protect it against attack."

The process of fortification is very fascinating in itself and is much more in depth than many may think. It is also quite revelatory. Iron in its natural state is a very weak material, and in order for it to become hardened, it has to be heated, and then have other materials added to it in a process called bonding. The main mineral that is added to the iron ore is called carbon. Now, the process through which these materials are brought together is called smelting. Smelting is when a material or materials are put in a blast furnace and heated until they are broken down into a liquid and pliable state. After this, the metal is allowed to cool naturally and slowly. This process is called "tempering," where the iron (which is now steel) is reheated and then allowed to cool naturally. This is done to allow the steel to expand and become denser but more flexible at the same time. All of this process makes the steel stronger, less brittle, and able to endure much more stringent poundings and force.

Most people don't know the difference between steel that has been tempered and steel that has been cooled by a process called "quenching." You see, both of them have gone through the same bonding and smelting process, but the difference is in how they are cooled. Where tempered steel is taken through a slow process of cooling, quenched steel is cooled instantly as soon as it has been cast. That's why they call it "cast iron," because although it is steel, as soon as it has been poured into a mold, it is submerged in water and cooled immediately. This process makes the steel extremely hard, but it also makes it very inflexible, so it is subject to break if it is pounded too hard or dropped from too great a distance. Because it was cooled instantly rather than going through a cooling process, the steel has not been allowed to expand, and though it is dense, it has a greater propensity to break, because it is brittle.

It was amazing to me, as I researched what makes steel fortified, that I saw that it is much like people. We are much like iron ore, in that we have the potential to be extremely strong, but in our natural state, we are weak. Therefore, we must have a bonding agent added to us, and then be sent through a firing process, so that we can become fit for the steelworker's use. I didn't mention it earlier, but the part of carbon that is added to the ore is one percent. Isn't that ironic? I say that because, as human beings, we are all carbon-based organisms, and it takes God to be the ninety-nine percent, and us to be the one percent, in order to get things accomplished.

The most revelatory aspect was in the cooling process, which gives the very ability to be fortified. What I saw was that the ability to become something great was all in the cooling process, not in the actuality of being poured or cast into something. It appeared to me that being tempered will allow us to become fortified, so that we can be heated and reshaped into any tool or weapon that God would have us to be, because of the flexibility and strength that is forged in us when we take our time to become steel. The Word says in 2 Timothy 2:21: *"If a man therefore purge himself from these, he shall be a vessel unto honor, sanctified, and meet for the master's use, and prepared unto every good work"* (KJV).

Tempering is the process of patience, and in being tempered, we will lack nothing and can be used in any situation. However, quenched steel is not so, because it is only capable of doing or being one thing. Have you ever seen a cast-iron skillet fall on a tiled floor? It will crack it, and usually put a dent in it if it doesn't shatter the tile into pieces. But have you ever seen anyone drop a cast-iron skillet, or any other piece of quenched steel, on a concrete floor? What usually happens is the object will break upon impact. That's because, unlike tempered steel, iron that has been quenched has no flexibility. Therefore, it cannot be pounded on, dropped, or endure any form of battle. We as human beings fall into those two categories.

Now back to the armor. Your armor isn't just your outer shield; it's who and what you are spiritually and emotionally. Honestly speaking, in this day and time, how many of us expect to get involved in a confrontation where real armor is needed? Chances are you won't, but armor is actually more than just protection from physical attacks. When building your kingdom, you will suffer attacks from spiritual, emotional, and soulish enemies.

The key to withstanding them successfully is to ensure that you have been fortified. Have you ever had attacks made against your character, and instead of addressing them, you turned and ran? Well, nine times out of ten, God was trying to fortify your armor and your resolve. I am not saying that you should get in messy confrontations, but during times like those, there should be a courage in you that says, "I can withstand this, because I know who I am, and more so, who God is in me."

The Word of God says in Ephesians 6:13: "*Wherefore take unto you the whole armor of God, that ye might be able to withstand in the evil day and having done all to stand*" (KJV). What that says to me is, put on your armor, and make sure that it's fortified, because you are going to come up against it, but in the midst, be strong, because you are fortified. Undoubtedly, attacks will come, and they are almost certain to come unexpectedly, but understanding how to fortify your armor is the key to your survival.

Fortification comes first, in the renewing of your mind. It is there that you have the opportunity to prove God's will, which is really your true armor. Secondly, your fortification is found in your prayer life. Philippians 4:6-7 says, "*Be anxious for nothing; but in everything by prayer and supplication with thanksgiving let your requests be made known unto God. And the peace of God, which passes all understanding, shall keep your hearts and minds through Christ Jesus*" (KJV2000). Peace is the greatest fortifier any armor can have. Without peace while warring in a battle, you may as well give up. Prayer will give you God's peace.

The next fortification tool is found in worship. It is in worship that you get into or access the presence of God, and in battles or trials, if God's presence is not with you, then, as we say where I'm from, "you burnt up." 1 Peter 4:12 speaks about being tried by fire. It says: "*Beloved, think it not strange concerning the fiery trial which is to try you, as though some strange thing happened to you*" (KJV).

Let me take it even further to convince you of my findings. In the third chapter of Daniel, the story of the three Hebrew boys is told. It is about how they refused to worship King Nebuchadnezzar's golden image god, telling the king that they would only worship the True and Living Most High God. Well, if you don't know the story, then read it, but to summarize things, the three were cast into a furnace that was heated seven times hotter than it normally was. As a matter of fact, it was so hot that the men who put them in the furnace died from the heat. Well, upon looking and watching the fire and the boys, Nebuchadnezzar asked, "Did we not put three into the furnace?" and one of his elders said, "Yes, King, it is true." Then the king said, "Then why do I see four walking around in the flames, and the fourth looks like the son of God?" Needless to say, the Hebrew boys were not harmed, nor did they smell like smoke when they exited. My point is, worship fortifies you so much that it not only brings you into the presence of God, but it brings God into your presence.

In order for your armor to be fortified, you have to be willing to be cast into fiery situations and trials. It is only through fire that anything can be heated enough to become stronger. If God is not in your smelting process, then you may be used to the fire, but adding God makes your armor strong for battle, and He'll temper you. If God isn't in your process, you may be hard, but when the battle comes, you'll find that your armor is brittle, and you'll break.

4. Are There Chinks in Your Armor?

This question holds significant relevance, as it denotes the ability of one who desires to become, remain, and successfully continue to be king, and to be in kingship. The term "chink in the armor" refers to the ability to be attacked, and/or to having weak points. These two definitions are from the Urban Dictionary:

1) A narrow opening and vulnerable area in one's armor that an enemy will usually aim for.

2) A figurative term for one's weakness, largest flaw, or their prevention of success.

Failure to accomplish your destiny doesn't necessarily mean that you have a chink or chinks in your armor, but it does mean that whatever is wrong, you just refuse to get it fixed, or even address or acknowledge that a problem exists.

Chinks, as it relates to your quest to gain kingship or royalty, aren't the actual holes in your armor. No, it's the weakness of not addressing your character flaws, moral deficiencies, psychological issues, and spiritual dilemmas. Many times, in battle, your enemy will attack your weakest point, and as I was told in my formative years in sports, "a chain is only as strong as its weakest link." So, it stands to reason that you're only as strong as your character, morals, psychological fitness, and spiritual grounding.

The thing about finding out if you have chinks in your armor is that you cannot see them while you are in your armor. You either have to remove it and examine it yourself or have someone you trust tell you where there are flaws or holes. Now, the thing about me is, I have never been one to allow someone to inspect my property or equipment without watching them inspect it, because I always think that they may miss something. The only one you can truly trust to do an accurate assessment of your armor is God, and that's through the Holy Spirit.

However, understand that even when it is determined that you have chinks, then you'll still have to surrender your armor to be fixed. Trusting anyone to fix something of yours (even when it's not operating correctly) can be very difficult. That's because we learn to function and make adjustments for the thing not operating properly. But please understand that when we operate that way, we are setting ourselves up for failure. This is because your enemy is always looking for ways to infiltrate your life and your success, and he has already pinpointed where you are weak and how he will attack you. God created you with perfectly operating armor, but through life's battles, it may become damaged.

The first step in repairing your armor is surrendering it. It is impossible to have your armor fixed while you're still in possession of it or wearing it. The reason why is that the blacksmith first cleans the armor, then cuts out the damaged part of the iron or steel. It's very difficult to repair the breach with the damaged armor still there, because the damaged armor is weak and not fit for battle, and new welded steel will not adhere to or bond with damaged armor.

After the damaged metal has been cut away, new steel is poured from the inside, because it can be shaped into the form of the armor without revealing the damage. The molten steel not only has to cover the cut away portion but has to adhere to the existing metal; if it is poured outwardly, then you can see where the damage was, and a good blacksmith will never allow damage to be detected.

Next, the steel is allowed to cool, but all the while, it is being shaped while it is in its softest form, because it has to be molded, shaped, and contoured to the existing armor. After this, it is grinded, pounded, and tested to see if the spot or spots can hold up to the pounding of battle. Then and only then, after it is deemed sufficient, is it finished, polished, and returned to its wearer for battle.

God cannot allow us to go into battle with chinks in our armor, because the enemy knows where they are. Why? Because he put them there, and it would be extremely foolish to go into battle against an enemy that knows all of your weak spots. No, surrender your armor, and allow the blacksmith or armorer to repair it and make it battleworthy, because if you don't, then you will never reach your throne. By the way, you do realize the blacksmith and armorer are God and the Holy Spirit, right? I'm just checking!

What and Who Are You Fighting For?

There has never been a battle fought for which there was no purpose. Even before man was created, there was a battle fought in heaven: it was waged by Lucifer against God, to take over heaven and God's throne. Every war, battle, fight, and skirmish was, is, and forever will be fought to gain land, money, resources, religious ideals, freedom from tyranny, and worst of all, foolish pride. The key is to understand if it is necessary to fight, or if it would be better to negotiate. However, if it is necessary to fight, then you must understand the following questions: what are you fighting for, who is your enemy, what is at stake, do you have the resources to sustain a war, who are your allies, who are the allies of your enemy, and most important, are you prepared to go to war?

In this day and time, unless you are a country or a nation, then you won't be fighting physical battles. These days, most wars are fought in boardrooms, courtrooms, and last but not least (by any stretch of the imagination), in the spirit realm. Not everything that has significance is just about money, land, and power, and it's not just about your potential kingdom either. It is about the souls of men, and as it was in the beginning, so shall it be in the end.

Being successful in battle is not just about having brilliant strategies. No, as important as strategy is, it is not the determining factor for success. The determining factor for potential success in each battle you fight is reconnaissance. According to Webster's Dictionary, "reconnaissance" means "a military observation of a region to locate an enemy or ascertain strategic features."

Anything or anyone that you are in opposition with, you should have proper intelligence on them if you expect to defeat them. Every successful sports organization on earth has what you call "scouts." Whether it's Pop Warner football, the NFL, the NBA, or MLB, every successful team scouts their opponents, and most professional organizations spend millions of dollars each year just to get a winning edge.

It is no different in the spirit realm, because the devil is constantly doing "recon." 1 Peter 5:8 says, "*Be sober, be vigilant; because your adversary the devil, as a roaring lion, walks about, seeking whom he may devour*" (KJV2000). Well, if he does it, then shouldn't we? 2 Corinthians 2:11 says, "*Lest Satan should get an advantage of us: for we are not ignorant of his devices*" (KJV). There is an axiom that says, "We should see the devil from afar." This simply means that we can understand what the enemy is doing without getting close to him.

In the book of Numbers, beginning with the thirteenth chapter, Moses sent out twelve spies to spy on the land of Canaan. Ten of the twelve spies came back with reports of fear and doom, but Caleb and Joshua came back with reports saying that they could take the land, and that they were well able. It is important not to let the spirit of fear affect your "scouting report," and even those you send out to do reconnaissance (if you don't do it yourself) should have your mind and vision. If not, you are destined to lose your battle.

Understanding what you are fighting for – and, in particular, *whom* – is even more paramount. I say this because, if you aren't invested in your heart in what you are fighting for, then you stand a greater chance of defeat. In Genesis 29:20, the scripture reads, "*So Jacob served seven years for Rachel and they seemed to him but a few days because of his love for her*" (NASB). Later, in the chapter, you'll find that Jacob was fooled into marrying Leah, Rachel's sister, by their father Laban. You'll see that Jacob then worked an additional seven years to acquire Rachel's hand in marriage, because he was passionate about her and had to have her at all cost. Even if it cost him fourteen years of his life, Jacob deemed her worth it. For this very reason, the phrase was coined: "a man labors for that which he loves."

In going to war, one must identify if the person or thing they are fighting for is worth dying for. If it isn't, then don't fight, because you aren't equipped for battle. 2 Timothy 2:4 states: "*No man that wars entangle himself with the affairs of this life; that he may please him who has chosen him to be a soldier*" (KJV2000). What are you willing to fight for? Is it your faith, your job, your freedom, your wife, or your kids? But an even more important question is, what are you willing to die for? Are you willing to sacrifice for the things that you love? Is your recreation time more important than praying for your marriage that is failing, or your children who are being pulled into worldly distractions, or your very soul? The question is, are you? Because you'd better believe that your adversary is, and he is always ready to fight, because he desires to sift you as wheat.

1. What Are the Conditions of Your Battles?

I sort of alluded to this topic earlier, as it related to selecting your weapons of warfare. Understanding your conditions of battle is vitally important, because it will help you determine what type of strategy you should employ. In the military, as I stated earlier, everything is done according to battle conditions. Every aspect of battle is related to the conditions. They determine how you dress, how you fight, what you eat, when you sleep, and even what type of artillery and ammunition you use. I stated before that I am a high school football coach. I also played high school and college football. Now, during my time as a player, I was oblivious of my conditions. I dressed the same most of the time, even on cold and rainy days, and I wore the same shoes to practice and play games in. However, I never realized how inclement weather affected my play, and the field conditions caused me to be less successful in my outcomes. Why? Because, regardless of the conditions, I played the same way. I didn't adapt to my conditions or environment and didn't make adjustments to how I approached my opponent, and as a result, I lost some battles.

Fast-forward twenty-five plus years.... As a head football coach, it was my responsibility to pay attention to every detail of how my team practiced, prepared, and dressed, and even what type of shoes they wore. Unless you've played a field sport, e.g., football, baseball, soccer, or track and field, you don't know that you can't wear certain shoes on certain surfaces. In particularly wet conditions, you also have to wear extra-long studs on your cleats, because regular half-inch cleats don't dig into the ground deep enough to get adequate footing. Even your play calling is based on the conditions. If it's windy, then you don't throw long passes, and if it's muddy, then you try and run to the grassier parts of the field.

I don't have any military experience, but I do know that conditions dictate your battle strategies. For example, if you are facing attacks against your children, then you don't pray against the spirit of covetousness, and if finances are being attacked, then you don't come against the spirit of rejection. What I am saying is, always understand what your surroundings are. This way, you will always know how to address your adversary, even if you have to fight him on his own turf.

2. Where Are Your Battles Taking You?

As I previously stated, no battle or war is fought without purpose or goal. Many battles are fought just to seize a stronghold whose acquisition will be pivotal in determining the outcome of a war. However great or small, battles are key in determining a war's outcome. But while winning a war is predicated upon winning key battles, understand, as it has been said, that "you can win the battle and yet lose the war." What that says to me is that you must choose carefully the battles that you engage in, and always predetermine if they are necessary in accomplishing your objective. You must always ask yourself, "What is driving me to fight this battle? If I win, what will I have gained, and if I lose, what will I have lost?"

Every battle should have an aiming point to gain advantage or give you a vantage point that brings you closer to your goal. There should never be any such thing as wasted time or energy, because both are things that you can never reclaim. The focus of your battle shouldn't just be motivated by acquiring your goal, but it should always be fueled by your passion, because passion never lets you become complacent. Your passion is what spurns you to greatness, and it allows you to exceed expectations of just obtaining your goal. A person who is only dedicated to achieving a goal, but doesn't have passion, will find that once they achieve that goal, they will be stuck and empty. That's because passion never allows you to stop.

Passion is what drove Jesus to become our sacrifice for sin, and it's what continues to drive him even today. What, you don't believe me? Well, read Hebrews 7:25, for it says, *"Therefore He is also able to save forever those who come to God through Him, since He ever lives to make intercession for them"* (NASB). If Jesus' passion had stopped at Calvary, then we would be in a sad state of affairs, but it didn't. Jesus' whole purpose is to make intercession for us. So, it's his passion that gives him purpose past that point, and it has to be ours as well.

Many people misquote this next scripture and use it out of context. That scripture is Matthew 11:12, which says, *"From the days of John the Baptist until now the kingdom of heaven suffers violence, and the violent take it by force"* (NKJV). What it means is that men have used their authority to gain position in the church, but "the violent" means passionate people who will stop at nothing to gain God's kingdom and his righteousness, and those are the ones who will always triumph over one with an agenda. It is passion that made the march on the bridge in Selma, Alabama, a day noted in history.

There is a Greek word "Biazoê," which literally means to overpower by forcefully rushing into. In order to get to where it is that God wants you to go, or that you want to go, there has to be Biazoê, or an overpowering force from within. If you don't allow your passion to drive you in the pursuit of your next goal, level, or place of destiny, then you will always miss your mark. Your obtaining is always found in your press, your destiny is in your decidedness. I have never seen anyone with a "meh" attitude reach their destiny. God will not honor you either, because He said in Revelation 3:16, *"So, because you are lukewarm, and neither hot nor cold, I will spit you out of my mouth"* (ESV). You will never reach your destiny being passive or lethargic; that will only get you a spectator's seat to watch the battle.

3. Is Your Battleground a Familiar Place?

In athletics, there is such a thing as having "home field advantage." This term refers to one team having an upper hand because where they play is their home stadium, and because of the consistency that they play there, they are comfortable. Most teams have winning records on their home court or field. However, every now and then, they experience defeat at the hands of a team who was better prepared, better physically, or just outright more talented than they were on that particular night. They may face each other numerous times on each other's home court, and sometimes they may split a series of contests, or one team might sweep the series. Ah, but if both teams make it to the playoffs, then it becomes a different scenario, because it is very difficult to beat a team in the playoffs that you have already beaten consistently. Why? Because the losing team is familiar with the winning team's style, methods, physicality, rhythm, and so on.

Familiarity is a very good thing, especially when it comes to battles and opponents. There is a saying, "Familiarity breeds contempt," and this is true, especially for the one who wins the majority of the time. This is because the one who wins most usually starts to develop an arrogance and an attitude that says, "We've got your number," and it deters that team from preparing sufficiently, or from taking the other team as seriously as they would a lesser or unfamiliar opponent. This is usually a good thing for the losing team, because it makes the team that wins consistently feel that they don't have to become innovative to beat the other team, and they have little concern for the other team's ability to innovate.

How many of you remember the 1991 Chicago Bulls championship season? Well, their nemesis was the Detroit Pistons, and the Pistons were the two-time defending world champions. The Bulls won the season series 3-2, but the Pistons felt that they had the Bulls' number, because for the previous three years, the Pistons basically annihilated the Bulls in the playoffs. But, as I said before, familiarity breeds contempt. Before the 1991 NBA Eastern Conference Championship, the Pistons had it in their minds that it would be business as usual, and they didn't think that they had to improve their level of play, but the Bulls knew that they had to up their own. Well, the Pistons didn't, and the Bulls did, and the result was a four-game sweep of the Pistons, with the Bulls winning their first of six NBA championships the following series.

I gave that example because I felt it was a great scenario to show how familiar conditions and battles can help one entity and hurt the other. Sometimes, it's a good thing to get beat up, or to lose repeatedly to someone who, for lack of a better choice of words, "bullies you," because either you are going to lie down and take the whipping, or you are going to find a way to defeat them. I've had my share of fights growing up, and early on I got beat up, but every person I fought repeatedly, I eventually ended up winning against, and one hundred percent of the time, that was our last fight. You see, once your opponent/bully finds out that you can beat them, and beat them decidedly, they usually don't want to fight anymore.

I heard a saying growing up: "You can't know where you're going if you don't know where you've been." Well, I used to think it was something cool and slick to say, but God gave me such a revelation of it. He showed me that everyone is given tests in life, and many times when we do poorly on a test or assignment, He allows it to be so, because it prepares us to win not just that round, but the next as well. You see, God is the Master of giving wisdom, insight, and understanding, and He allows us to gain them from our mistakes. If you are wise, then you will look at where or how you failed a test or trial, and no matter how the questions change, you realize that it's the same test, because you are familiar with the material. So, knowing where you erred teaches you how to avoid that error the next time, which means you can now get past that opponent and win that battle.

It should never be old opponents that trip you up, no matter who or what they may be. In the book of Ecclesiastes (1:9), Solomon said, *"There is nothing new under the sun."* That is so true, and I challenge you to do this the next time you have a dilemma. Ask yourself, "Have I seen this before, and who or what was it dressed as?" If you do this, then you will emerge victorious.

I had an older guy tell me something when I was much younger. His name was James "Mo" Armstrong, and he is since deceased, but I mentioned him by name because he would always give me wisdom for life and sport, and this is my way of honoring him. He said, "Elray, the game never changes, only the players do, and if you've seen it once, then you'll see it again." And so will you – just pay attention.

4. Do You Have a Battle Strategy and Plan for Success?

The most successful people in life have a strategy or plan, and they follow it to the letter, because they know that on the road to victory, there is no such thing as shortcuts. I had a coach in high school whose name is Glenn Johnson. He has won state championships in both boys' and girls' track twice. He has also won an IHSA state football championship, and he is also a member of the IHSA and National Coaches Hall of Fame for football and track. I mention him because he would always say, "Plan your work, work your plan, and your plan will work." It certainly has worked for him, and it has given me success in the areas where I have adhered to that philosophy. He would always talk about specificity of motion, and that you had to be over-intentional in your repetition, as he would say, "Practice makes permanent, but only perfect practice makes perfect." Sometimes in practice, he would say that we would only have to run one play twenty-five times, and then we could go home. However, that meant twenty-five times without a mistake. Well, that twenty-five times turned into 104 times before we ran twenty-five without a mistake, but in the playoff game that we ran it in, the other team couldn't stop it.

Again, every battle has to have a strategy or plan, because success is not haphazard or circumstantial, only winning the lottery is. Even before you develop your plans for battle, you must make sure that your troops are disciplined, even if you are the only one. It is impossible to fulfill or carry out a battle plan without training those carrying it out for battle. In the military, soldiers learn to march in step for the majority of boot camp, because it teaches the unit to move as one, and in conjunction and coordination with each other's movement.

Also, it is done with the mindset that at all times every man, to a person, should be in unison and not break formation. Remember, as I said earlier, a chain is only as strong as its weakest link. The training is in line with the thought to never break ranks and never deviate from the plan. Military life, just like championship teams, always start with the fundamentals, and they emphasize them continuously, because it is proven that when all else fails, you can always count on your basics.

As I said before, there is no shortcut to success. Every great strategist loves to see his opponent take shortcuts, because many times when you don't follow the prescribed plan, you leave yourself vulnerable. Many wars are lost because someone took a shortcut in battle and didn't follow the prescribed plan. In most cases, the unit or team that follows the plan will win the war, because if you follow the plan or strategy, then you'll leave no stone unturned. It's when you try and circumvent the process that you open yourself up to surprise attack or to being snuck up on. But when you do your due diligence and follow the course, you see every road and avenue to your destination, and you cannot be snuck up on, because you have cleared the brush.

Be very wary of people who always try and take shortcuts or circumvent processes and procedures, because they will always miss something vital to their success (and yours), and they will always end up lacking. As a football coach, I always started my players off with making sure their footwork drills were proper, because if your feet are bad, then everything else will be as well, because the feet are the foundation, and I have never seen anything last that was built on a bad foundation. It wasn't until I was satisfied that their foundations were stable that we even touched position fundamentals, and then we started learning plays.

I promise you that if you abandon your plans or strategies for success, or worse, your foundations, then you are setting yourself up for failure. Sure, situations arise where you have to make adjustments, but if you have to, you build on your foundation. Its fine to tweak ideas, but at the end of the day, ask yourself, "What do I (or we) do well?" and you build your plan on that, not on what someone else does, because you have no control over that.

Please, always remember that if you start at six, seven, eight, and nine, and someone stops you, then you have nowhere to go, because you didn't start at one, two, three, four, and five. Your plans should have short-term goals that turn into long-term success. This is proven in the book of Isaiah 28:10, because it says, "*For precept must be upon precept, precept upon precept; line upon line, line upon line; here a little, and there a little*" (KJV). This scripture is saying, take it slow, check your work, and make sure everything lines up, and that's how a plan is formulated. Even in writing this book, there was no great big epiphany. No, I had ideas that became more ideas, but it all started with a foundation.

There is a song that's called "Hold to God's Unchanging Hand," and the lyrics in the first verse say:

> "*Time is filled with swift transition.*
> *Naught of earth unmoved can stand.*
> *Build your hopes on things eternal.*
> *Hold to God's unchanging hand.*"

Truer words have never been spoken. The songwriter in her wisdom is saying that things will change swiftly, and nothing on earth will go unaffected by time and change, but there are things and principles that will not change, and these truths should be what you formulate your plans and strategies on. So hold to the principles of God, because they never change, and they never will!

5. Do You Understand Who or What Your Enemy Is?

The Cambridge Dictionary defines an enemy as "a person who hates or opposes another person and tries to harm that person. Dictionary.com gives this definition: "a person who feels hatred for, fosters harmful designs against, or engages in antagonistic activities against another; an adversary or opponent." However, I have my own definition of an enemy, and it is this: "anyone or anything that tries to obstruct or distract you from your goal or deter you from your destiny."

An enemy doesn't have to be a person who intentionally tries to keep you from reaching your goal. No, an enemy can be someone who truly loves and cares about you. There are two different types of enemies: hostile and unintentional. A hostile enemy is someone who deliberately intends to oppose you and deter you from achieving your goals or your destiny. An unintentional enemy is someone who unknowingly, and/or without malice or deliberation, attempts to keep you from reaching your God-appointed assignment, however good their intentions may be.

I want you to fully understand that not every person who opposes you is your enemy. Neither is every person that tries to help you or wish you well your ally. Sometimes, the person that you feel is trying to undermine you is actually your biggest ally, and not everything that averts or opposes you is an adversary.

Sometimes, people and entities that impede your progress are actually the hands of God, keeping you from the hands of disaster. If you are doing everything right, as it relates to the Word of God, then you have to ask yourself a very pertinent question, like: Am I going too fast? Do I have everything I need to sustain me once I get there? And am I mature enough to manage my destiny right now? I repeat, not everyone who opposes you means you harm, just as not every person who tries to help you is a friend.

That brings me to this point. Not every person who says "I'm with you," or is your cheerleader, is your ally. There are quite a few scriptures of reference that support this statement. One in particular is Proverbs 27:6, which says, "*Wounds from a friend can be trusted, but an enemy multiplies kisses*" (NIV). Just because someone opposes you, it does not necessarily mean they aren't for you, just as one who promotes you is not necessarily really on your side. Case in point, in Matthew 16:22-23, it talks of Jesus telling His disciples that soon He would be offered up, at which point Peter said, "*Never, Lord! This shall never happen to you!*" It was then that Jesus said, "*Get behind me, Satan! You are a stumbling block to me; you do not have in mind the concerns of God, but merely human concerns*" (NIV). Was Peter Jesus' enemy? Of course, he wasn't, but his love for Jesus had his affections misplaced, concerning Jesus' purpose.

Like Jesus did, we must be in constant communication with God, so that you can always know your purpose, and your – or should I say God's – timing. Understanding your season, timing, and destiny will help you identify people who are purposeful in the execution of your destiny. Knowing who you are, and what you were created to do and be, will help you determine your roadblocks. Understanding when it is your season to arrive will help you identify your enemies, be they hostile or friendly.

6. Are You Acting as Your Own Enemy?

Most times, it is relatively easy to identify your enemies, especially when you understand what your destiny or goal is. This is simplified even further when they expose themselves as hostile or friendly. However, understanding or identifying when you are your own enemy is very difficult. This is because it is always easier to look at things outwardly, as opposed to looking introspectively.

It is extremely difficult to look at yourself and identify your shortcomings, because it takes a great deal of honesty, humility, and most of all, courage. The most ironic thing is, if you don't have these attributes, you've just found your enemies. They are the lack of character, lack of discipline, and lack of integrity. I say that because, if you lack the first three, then you'll definitely have the last three.

Identifying if you are acting as your own enemy requires you to look at your own life, retrospectively, and then determine where you failed or missed the mark. Once you have determined where, then you must determine how and why, after which you must identify what and who. This is especially difficult, because it requires a characteristic that you may not yet possess: honesty. However, if you can muster up the honesty to identify those things, then you will need the courage to answer the most important question: who or what was the common denominator in your failure? If you identify that it was you, then you are the culprit, and your own enemy.

I'm reminded of *The Andy Griffith Show*, and especially the character Barney Fife. The character never saw himself as he was, and never identified that he was the problem most of the time, an unintentional enemy. In particular, he was a sheriff's deputy, but he always carried an empty gun, and he was made to carry his one bullet in his shirt pocket. This was because he was always discharging his weapon in its holster, and thus labeled dangerous. The point that I am trying to make is, although he was given authority, office, and power, he couldn't act in the fullness of that authority or power, because his carelessness and lack of responsibility made him his own enemy. The thing is, he wasn't just a danger to himself, but also to those around him. Although he was given power and authority to administrate order, he couldn't act in the fullness of his office. You see, without his weapon, he became a liability to those around him, who needed him to protect them. If you act as your own enemy, not only will you not reach your true destiny, but you are at risk of letting other people down, and possibly responsible for them not reaching their own destinies.

It isn't until you become completely transparent with yourself and deal with the "Man in the Mirror" with what I call the "Butt-Naked" truth, popping the pimples of self-deception, that you will be able to grow into the fullness that God has for you and walk into the destiny that He has awaiting you. If you don't do these things, then you will always walk around unprepared, and you will never be fully empowered to be what you have been called to be, and to do what you have been called to do: serve in excellence. How can you serve in excellence without being fully equipped to do so? Acting as your own enemy will only put you in situations in which you are given keys of authority, but you wind up imprisoning yourself in that authority because you mishandle the keys. Don't get locked up in authority that you were meant to master. In other words, don't be a Barney Fife

Chapter III

Dressing

Understanding Why You Dress

In today's society, the detail and even desire to dress has lost its appeal. Up until about ten years ago, there was an unwritten dress code for everything, and it ranged from school to church, from job interviews to parties, etc. It appears that over the last decade or two, the attention to not just dressing, but dressing with class has lost its allure. There was a time even in the early to mid-twentieth century when men and women wore suits, ties, and dresses to sporting events. However, in this age of humanism, and "do what you feel," the dress code has been lost. Even in the church, where folk put on their "Sunday best," the attire has gone from suits and dresses to jeans with holes in them, tights as pants, and form-fitting dresses that garner the name Distraction.

I mention the attire in church, because that is where dress codes truly began. In the twenty-eighth chapter of Exodus, it was there that God first directed His priests on how to dress to enter into the Holy of Holies and the Tent of Meeting. He even gave direction down to what colors and materials, and in what way and how many times things were to be tied. That was because everything done had a purpose and was part of a ceremonial experience to enter into the presence of God.

The key word in that sentence is "ceremony." You see, everything that is done that has any significance is done with some form of ceremonial process, ranging from graduations to baptism and from courtrooms to funerals. Ceremonies are pertinent and necessary in every arena of life, because they dictate and denote structure, order, and advancement or elevation, and in each ceremony, there is always some code of dress. These dress codes are necessary to mark distinction, and further to validate that the event is not ordinary.

Now back to the priest and God's specific orders for entrance into His presence. It seems to me that if God had requirements for priests to dress with a certain degree of excellence, and not haphazardly or "run of the mill," then it would appear to me that He still does. I say this because He has never given an order for the priests who ministered unto Him to stop. If that is so, then it stands to reason that it is still a requirement. After all, aren't we called, even commanded to be a royal priesthood? Well, that means that we are continually called to be kings and priests, and therefore, when we minister unto the Lord and enter into His presence ceremonially, we should be appropriately dressed. I am not saying that we have to wear suits and dresses in everything that we do, but if the occasion has an element of ceremony to it, then shouldn't one dress accordingly?

The correct way to determine how to dress is to determine what type or degree of ceremony it is. I mean, at the Academy Awards and Grammy presentations, tuxedos and evening gowns are the required attire. At graduation ceremonies, the graduates wear caps and gowns. At military or law enforcement training graduations, the entire graduating class is required to dress in their formal dress attire. Even in the book of Revelation, it speaks of the ceremony when Jesus is named King of Kings: His crown and apparel are brought forth, and His wardrobe changes.

If we can dress for life's significant ceremonies, and honor man with the symbolism of our dress changing to represent a new level of life, then every time we come into the presence of God in His sanctuary, then we should – no, we are required to – dress as and be kings and priests. If nothing else, coming into the presence of God symbolizes that we have gone from a dead and lowly state to a state of newness of life, and there is no greater ceremony than that, nor any greater honoree.

I know that some of you may think that it doesn't take all of that, but it really does, and I'm not just talking about the aspect of church. Everyday living also has edicts and dictates for how you should dress. Walk into a prestigious law firm with blue jeans on for a job interview, and I guarantee that you will be shown the door. How you dress is important, because it not only speaks of how you esteem yourself, but it also shows to what extent you esteem other people.

What Does Your Wardrobe Say About You?

In essence, your wardrobe says one of two things about you: either you get it, or you don't. Either you're ready for the opportunity, or you're not. Either you understand the moment, or it's too big for you. Your clothing is the first thing anyone sees or is presented with concerning your character. So, if you show up to an interview, and your clothes are wrinkled and your shoes are run over and unpolished, then the general impression of the interviewer will probably be that you are sloppy and don't pay attention to detail. Needless to say, you probably won't get the job.

Your wardrobe speaks volumes about your character, your maturity, and your understanding, even before you ever speak a word. You see, people make up their minds based on how you look, before they come to any conclusion about what you say. It is said, "You don't get a second chance to make a first impression." People will see how you look before they find out how you smell, how you sound, or even how your intelligence comes across. Have you ever been somewhere and seen a person who was dressed quite poorly, but you find out later that that person was very wealthy? Well, most wealthy people don't dress up much, because they don't have anything to prove, but I'm sure that they know how to dress appropriately for venues.

As I spoke about first impressions in the previous paragraph, I'll use the old cliché, "A first impression is a lasting one." In all actuality, you can be totally outclassed and severely underqualified for certain opportunities and positions, but your wardrobe will get you an opportunity at least to get an introduction, just as the opposite is true. Have you ever seen someone who was impeccably dressed, and you thought that they held a much higher position than you anticipated? Or have you ever been in for an interview and found out that the worst-dressed person there was actually the company's president? Did it kind of change your mind about the company? Your wardrobe and how you dress says so much about you, and everyone likes to be around sharp-dressed people. Remember, your wardrobe says things about you that your mouth, resume, and recommendations could never get the opportunity to say.

What Is Your Purpose for Dressing?

Just about every person in the world has a destination or a job to do when they wake up. Everyone has a reason and purpose that they dress, even if it's for no other reason than to get the paper or go to the mailbox. However, every occupation has a code of dress, and it's usually to identify that person's position. It doesn't matter if you are a firefighter, police officer, postal carrier, doctor, chef, or even a professional athlete, everyone dresses with the purpose of being identified with their position and profession.

As it relates to your purpose for dressing, first, you have to identify where you are trying to go, and what you are trying to accomplish. Everything in Life has significance, and even in the book of Ecclesiastes, verse 9:11 ends with *"but time and chance happen to them all"* (NIV). What I think this scripture is saying is that every man has an opportunity for success, but when your time comes, can you seize the moment? Yes, everything in life has significance. The question is, what is yours? What is the purpose for which you deem it necessary to dress with skill and intent? 1 Corinthians 14:10-11 says:

"There are, it may be, so many kinds of voices in the world, and none of them is without signification. Therefore if I know not the meaning of the voice, I shall be to him that speaks a barbarian, and he that speaks shall be a barbarian to me." (AKJV)

This is about the purpose of tongues in the church. However, it applies to life as well, because it says that if you don't understand your purpose, then you are without significance, and if you can't understand your purpose, no one else can understand it either.

One day, when I was about twenty-three years old, my older cousin asked me what time it was. I told him that I didn't know, because I didn't have a watch. Then he told me something that changed my life forever. He said, "Then you're worthless." I asked why he would say such a thing, and he said, "Because a man without a watch has no purpose in life, because he doesn't have anywhere to be." Needless to say, the next day, I went out and bought a watch. What I am trying to say is, if you don't know your destinations in life, nor what season or time you should arrive, then you are without plan or purpose. If you don't have a purpose, then you'll never know how, why, when, where, or what to dress in or for. Unfortunately, as insignificant as it may seem, understanding the reason you dress is tied to where you are going in life, and if you don't know that, then it's going to be a bumpy ride on a rocky road, because, to quote Myles Munroe, "Where purpose is not known, abuse is inevitable," and who wants to follow a king who doesn't know where he's going?

Where Will Your Wardrobe Give You Access To?

I found myself unintentionally referring to the five W's in previous chapters. This is because, no matter what you do, these are questions that you need to ask yourself, either in formulating your plan for success or in figuring out how to solve problems once you get there. If you aren't aware of the meaning of the "Five W's," they are Who, What, Where, Why, and When. These five simple questions, if answered correctly, can lead to an unbelievably high degree of success in any endeavor. But the failure to consider any one of them can result in a disappointing reality, where you miss your goals, your dreams, and even your destiny. Understanding where your wardrobe will take you and give you access to is one of the first tools that you need to ensure your success.

Every venue has a dress code. Some are idealized, some are implied, and some are strict. The key to getting access is to be able to figure out and define what it takes to get in. Here is how the five W's come into play. First, let's start off with "What." What are you trying to accomplish and gain access for? If you don't know what your purpose of access is, then all your other W's will be moot points with little to no significance. "What" is the essence of everything that is occurring. So, if you don't know what you are gaining access for, then you will not have anything to substantiate the other W's. "What" has to tell you or give you a reason to change the way that you presented yourself previously.

Next is "Why." "Why" is your passion and motivation for even wanting access. "Why" gives you clarity or purpose, and it is what allows you to have vision in the first place. The question "Why?" should drive you to attain your next level and be your best self. Also, it should never just be about only you. If you have thoughts for the betterment of others, then "Why" will give you the wherewithal to endure ridicule, humiliation, discipline, and whatever sacrifice you have to, because there is more riding on your change than just your hopes.

"Where" is the next question that needs to be addressed. "Where" is the locator of your aspirations. This question is not only the determining factor of how to gain access to your goals, but also how far access can impact the success of your goals. Have you ever heard anyone say, "I never dreamed that I'd be here one day," or "I was at the right place at the right time"?

However, I want you to be fully aware that "Where" is not a "turkey shoot" or a rolling of the dice. "Where" is an exact place, and you need to research it or be instructed on the destination by someone who has been there. If you don't understand or have an idea of where the destination is, then access is futile, because gaining access to the wrong place can be more devastating to your goals than no place at all. If you haven't figured it out, prayer and God's direction are needed in all of these processes. The Holy Spirit is the ultimate GPS system, because Jesus said, *"He will lead and guide you in all truth"* (John 16:13).

Next, there is "When." "When" is as important a question as anything, because everything has an appointed time. In the book of Ecclesiastes 3 :1-3, Solomon writes these words:

> *"To everything there is a season, and a time to every purpose under the heaven: A time to be born, and a time to die; a time to plant, and a time to pluck up that which is planted; a time to kill, and a time to heal; a time to break down, and a time to build up..."* (KJV)

There are five more verses in that passage that you should read, and they give credence to the statement that everything has a time. Understanding "When" is actually more important than any of the other "W's," because even if you have all of the other ones on point, if you miss your appointed time, then all may be lost anyway. Have you ever missed a scheduled bus and had to wait for another, or gotten to a place of business right after they've closed? But the worst one to me is, have you ever gone somewhere at the right time, but on the wrong date? All of those things are very frustrating, because they have consequences as to where you go next. I've heard it said that "timing is everything." Well, that's true, especially when you're in God's timing.

The last of the five W's is "Who." "Who" is the God-appointed person or people who usher you to your future. You never walk into any service establishment and just seat yourself or go into a kitchen and start preparing your own meal. No, someone seats you, directs you to your table, or takes your order for your meal to be prepared. Well, understand this: neither do you just walk into your destiny. You have to be escorted by someone who knows the way.

Some may think that I went around the mulberry bush, but I really didn't. The five W's tie into your reason for dressing, because everything you do has purpose as to where you are going, what you hope to accomplish, why it needs to be that place, when you need to be there, and who will show you the way to get there and, once you arrive, the proper way to handle success.

However, understand, as I said in the beginning, every place of importance has a dress code. Some places have a "whatever you like" dress code, but others state that you must have a blazer and tie on in order to gain entrance. Your wardrobe dictates where you gain access to, because it says that either you belong, or you are inappropriately dressed. The five W's tell you what your plan should be before, during, and after you gain entry. Remember, even deliverymen and repairmen get access to certain establishments, but they only get back door access, and they're only there to drop off or service something. But proper wardrobe gives you access to the front door and all the amenities that your venue can afford you. If you can afford to be there, then you'll hear these words: "Right this way, your table is ready."

Are You Dressing for Your Present, or for Your Future?

I remember when I was a young man, there was a song by Eric B. and Rakim called "In the Ghetto." The song talked about the conditions of a person's surroundings, but also about how one could elevate their mind past their environment and lift themselves mentally, and as a result, change their conditions both immediately and in the future. The lead-in line after he talked about all the negativity of his environment, but about seeing himself in a better state, was "It's not where you're from, it's where you're at." I think there's quite a lot to be said about such a statement, because in essence, it's saying it doesn't matter where you start at, it only matters where you end up. I like to tweak it a little and say, "It's not where you're at, it's where you're going." Proverbs 29:18 says, "*Where there is no vision, the people perish...*" (KJV). This is true, because there is no way to move on to a place you cannot envision yourself in.

As the saying goes, "If you expect to get something you've never had, then you have to do something you've never done." This is true on so many levels, and it runs parallel to so many of life's edicts. It is virtually impossible to continue to dress as a painter and become a police officer after you've entered the academy. It is highly unlikely that you will ever become a doctor while dressing as a garbage man. No, in both instances, your mode of dress has to change, even as you go through the steps to become something new.

Becoming something first has to take place in the mind. In both instances, the people going through the trainings have to change the way they dress just to gain entry into the training facility. Then they are taught to see and think of themselves as what they'll become, not what they see. Even a bodybuilder starts off his training lifting lighter weights and changing his diet in hopes of becoming a bodybuilder; he has to change his immediate routine in order to accomplish his goals for the future.

As those in pursuit of a goal get closer to it, the way that they dress changes. In the police academy, your uniform changes as you get closer to being sworn in. You go from khakis to your actual uniform, then you go from no gun to a full duty belt, and then you get your emblems and badge that identify you as a sworn officer of the law. In medical school, your dress goes from plain clothes, to scrubs, to your lab coat, to your official white coat with "Doctor" in front of your name. A bodybuilder's dress changes by the degree of muscle he shapes and accumulates.

The thing is, if you don't dress appropriately for your future, you will never be taken seriously in your present. You cannot say that you want to be a lawyer but come to class every day dressed as a clown. You will never be taken seriously, and furthermore, you will run the risk of being dismissed from law school by the administration for being a distraction, no matter how potentially brilliant you may be.

There are rules both written and unwritten in this world, when it comes to getting access to your future. Case in point, my Apostle Dr. Matthew L. Stevenson III is the most anointed Man of God I've ever had the pleasure to witness. Not only is he one of the wisest and most insightful men I've met. He also has an actual doctorate in education, and he has held some lofty positions with our city's school board, all this being done as a very young man. The thing is, now the world is becoming – or should I say "has become" – aware of who he is and the anointings he possesses. When I first got to the ministry, he dressed and wore his hair like this generation known as "millennials," but over the last few months, he has changed his manner of dress and appearance. I think it is in large part due to his recognizing that his scope and notoriety have changed, and his influence has as well. Is he as anointed in skinny jeans and hoodies? Of course, he is. But the maturity in him realized that he'll reach more people the more seriously he is viewed. Sometimes, you have to sacrifice your wants to accommodate others' needs and learn to be comfortable being uncomfortable. Dressing is about access to your future and effecting necessary change. Always remember, "It's not where you're at, it's where you're going."

Don't Dress Because It's Popular, Dress Because It's Purposeful

Have you ever attended or watched an sporting event and seen a section of fans all wearing the home team's colors, but in the midst of those fans, you see a person or small group of people wearing the away team's colors or jersey? Have you ever said to yourself, "Wow, they have a lot of nerve being in that sea of fans dressed like that"? Well, you were right, they do have a lot of nerve, not just because they were wearing the other team's colors, but because they weren't afraid to make a statement. The act of dressing different was the voice saying, "I am not normal or status quo. I am different, and I dance to the beat of a different drummer."

Dressing according to popular standards is fine and being trendy is okay. But conformity usually won't get you noticed or pointed out in a crowd. However, the person who will dare to be different, and not just dress the way that everyone else does, is usually the one who is either ridiculed or celebrated – either way, they are noticed. A person who is not run of the mill is usually not afraid to go against the grain or stand out. It is these people who are declared by others to have style, and who usually become trendsetters. Trendsetters set the pulse of society and regulate or change its heartbeat. But have you ever realized that the ones who are celebrated for their style and become trendsetters are usually the same ones who were ridiculed for their style?

Anyone who dares to be different will often face opposition and ridicule. The reason is because people are creatures of comfort, consistency, and habit, and they get offended when someone adds color and pop to a rigid, unimaginative, and mundane way of life. It is the person who is not afraid to be or dress differently who is given a voice. We see it every day, and I can prove it. Do you remember when jeans were worn loosely and comfortably? But then "skinny jeans" hit the market, and I for one was offended at the idea of men and boys wearing their pants so tight. However, what was ridiculed and considered a shock and outrage has become a fashion industry norm, and today every aspect of fashion is influenced by it. All it takes to change opinion or culture is to get one person to emulate or copy your style, and before you know it, you've changed or set a trend.

The greatest trendsetter the world has ever seen didn't come just to be different, but came to change the culture because of purpose, and that trendsetter's name was Jesus Christ. Jesus' whole mission in life was to be different with His manner of dress, but His wardrobe was His life. Jesus came and wore the away team's jersey at the home team's game. I say this humorously, but didn't Jesus come to change the traditions of man, and even add pop and color, which are known as love and grace, to the rigid way of religion? Was He not ridiculed and humiliated because His style was different? But because someone dared to emulate and copy his style, a whole trend of "Christians" was created as a result of His being different, and He who was once ridiculed now is celebrated.

The transition to the spiritual was to get you to understand the importance of the purpose for which you dress. However,

Dressing

I don't want you to think for one second that Jesus wasn't a fashion changer. Jesus must have had some pretty fly, unique, and uncommon clothes, because it says that after He was crucified, the Roman soldiers cast lots (shot dice) for his garments. Ask yourself, who would want to gamble for a dead man's clothes if they weren't all that?

It has been said for quite some time that "the clothes make the man," and in some ways, that's true. However, I say, "Clothes define the man and express his intent." There is a reason that everything is done. There is a reason why you dress with distinction, or dress to the mundane. A person dresses with distinction because they want to stand out, be separate, and make a declaration that says, "You will notice me, because I have something to say." The person in the mundane or popular trend says, "I am happy being normal, because I don't have that much to say. I am not here to make waves, because I don't want attention drawn to me." Dressing purposefully will get you noticed, and once you are noticed, then I pray that you know your purpose. If you dress a certain way because it's how everyone else dresses, then I pray that purpose finds you, because when it does, it will change the way others see you and the way you see yourself.

Does Your Dress Inspire or Irritate?

There was a song by a group called The Persuaders entitled "Thin Line Between Love and Hate." This is very true concerning matters of the heart, and equally as true when it comes to matters of style and dress. There is a fine line between your style of dress inspiring someone and irritating someone. Have you ever been some place, and someone comes in with way too much cologne on? Usually, they get the response, "Dude, what do you have on?!" However, when someone with the same cologne comes in with the right amount on, they get the response, "Excuse me, sir, what is that fragrance that you have on, and where did you buy it?" Both were wearing the same cologne and were asked the same question. The difference is, one was asked out of irritation, and the other was asked due to inspiration. The difference is in understanding what is enough and what is too much.

The same is true when it comes to dressing. Have you ever seen someone with a really nice suit on, but the way that they accessorized was way too much, and as a result, it ruined the look? On the flip side of that, have you ever seen someone with the same suit on, and they did just enough, and you said in your mind, "Now that guy is sharp"? The key in both scenarios is knowing when to say "when." An accent piece or a pop of color goes a long way in bringing out the best in your ensemble. However, doing too much can take your look from chic to clownish. Monograms, handkerchiefs, shoes, ties, even a boutonniere can be the crowning pieces of an ensemble, but too much of them all, or too many color variations can kill a look. A monogram on a sleeve, cuff, or collar is an awesome accentuation, but you can't monogram everything – that is called overkill.

Let your dress say about you that you took the time to put your look together, but that you didn't overthink it, nor did you overdo it. A properly dressed man whose look inspires will always get a stare, a nod, or a compliment. A man who has done too much will get a glance and a dismissive look, because he has gone down the road of the irritant. It is far better to be looked over, than to be overlooked. Also, understand that less is more in some cases, and it's okay to leave someone's imagination working with what they could have done with the same outfit. It's fine to leave something to the imagination. As a man, I love it when I see a woman who is dressed alluringly but leaves something to the imagination, as opposed to one who leaves nothing to it.

It should be your intention to always be committed to a person's memory because of the way you're dressed, and it should be your desire to inspire them to "step up their game." Never dress in a fashion that dismisses you, because dismissal means disqualification, and if you're disqualified, then you have no seat.

Chapter IV

A Seat at the Table

What a Seat at the Table Means

A seat at the table means that you have been given admittance and access to the place where discussions are held, and decisions are made. It doesn't mean that you are given a voice to have a say, give input, or be asked for your insight in the decision-making proceedings, but it does mean that you are welcome to be privy to the discussions, and one day, you may have the opportunity to be a voice in the decision making. A seat at the table means just that: take a seat. In taking a seat, you should always understand that your initial objective is to learn.

Many people, when invited into the conversation, make the mistake of thinking that they have arrived, and thus are under the illusion that they have as much say as anybody else. If you are allowed to have a seat, then one day you will, but initially watch and learn the process, because just like you were invited to the table, you can be uninvited. The way that you gain a voice is to find a mentor, or let a mentor find you. If you stay attentive and present, and conduct yourself in an appropriate and respectful manner, then someone will come up to you and introduce themselves to you, and if they like, respect, and value you and what you have to say when you are asked a question, then they will introduce you to their friends, and then you will be in line to have a voice. Remember, a seat does you no good if no one acknowledges you once you're in it.

I was once told that rushing is a sign of immaturity. Being impetuous is a quick and sure way to destroy images and impressions. Everything is about access, opportunity, and voice, and if you are afforded those things, then you can make a difference in not only your life, but the lives of those who matter to you. After all, all that political arenas, offices, and appointments are is seats at the table. All politicians do is discuss, set, and make policies for the people who elect them. However, you never see a newly elected official come into office and immediately start demanding changes or setting policy. That's because that person has to learn the protocol of having a voice. Knowing the power of the seat, or the weight that the seat carries, should make one sober and humble in how they use it, because it has the ability to change lives, no matter how small the table may be, and that should be your only reason for wanting a seat.

A seat at the table gives you not only a place in the present, but a place in history as well. But, far more importantly and with much greater implications, a seat gives you an opportunity at creating legacy, and not only for your own generation, but for generations to follow. In my opinion, it should be everyone's desire to have a seat at the table, because it allows anyone in that seat to determine outcomes and affect lives through the authority and "say-so" that comes with it. Having a seat shouldn't just be an ambition or desire; it should be every person's responsibility to seek a seat on some level, and to be held accountable and hold the others sitting there accountable. It is only then that a seat at any table holds significance and value.

What Gives You a Seat at the Table?

There are three things that give you the potential to earn a seat at the table. I say "earn" because, while a seat can be bought, it is up to the others who have earned their position to eliminate the ones buying and selling chairs. Now, the three aforementioned things are commitment, consistency, and results. If you don't possess at least two of these three characteristics, then you are wasting not only your time, but the time of those sitting with you. Whatever is being discussed or determined at the table is serious and should only be discussed by serious people.

Those who sit at the table are usually the ones to determine who deserves a seat at the table, and the first attribute they look for is commitment. The word "commitment" means being dedicated to a cause, an activity, etc. The reason commitment is a quality that gets you a seat is because that quality shows people that you are passionate about something and will see it through. Many people profess to be committed to a cause, but irrefutably, the test of time will prove if you have stick-to-itiveness or not.

I remember when I was in my early thirties and helping to build my former ministry's new church. Well, quite a few of the men started out very dedicated, and I was one of them, but over the course of the next few months, the numbers of the men dwindled. Yes, it was hard work, but it was a labor of love. Well, ultimately, we got closer to being complete enough to move in, and as easier work started to be necessary, more and more men started to show back up. I didn't have issue with them showing up, or even saying they "built the church," because during the process, the wisest man I've ever met, the late Deacon Isaac Davis would say to me, "Ray, there are a whole lot of starters, but very few finishers." This would carry me through life in how I select people to participate in my projects, because I figured, if they don't show up for one important thing, they won't show up for another. The world and the people at the table do the same thing: they watch your commitment level in everything and choose accordingly. If you can't be committed to something other than your personal cause, then you probably aren't a committed person.

Next is consistency. Consistency has a few definitions, but I like a particular word and phrase. The word is "constant," and the phrase is "showing up to do your assignment always, no matter what the circumstances are." Consistency is the reason that streams become rivers, or that wars are won. It's because someone or something continues on until a change occurs, or a desired result comes to fruition. Another word for consistency is perseverance. Perseverance means to have steadfastness, regardless to the degree of difficulty or obstacles that you face in fulfilling your goal. There is a poem by Rudyard Kipling called "IF". The first and last stanzas of the poem say:

If you can keep your head   when all about you

Are losing theirs and blaming it on you,
If you can trust yourself
when all men doubt you,
But make allowance for their doubting too;
If you can wait and not be tired by waiting,
Or being lied about, don't deal in lies,
Or being hated, don't give way to hating,
And yet don't look too good, nor talk too wise;
If you can talk with crowds
and keep your virtue,
Or walk with Kings –
nor lose the common touch,
If neither foes nor loving friends can hurt you,
If all men count with you, but none too much;
If you can fill the unforgiving minute
With sixty seconds' worth of distance run,
Yours is the earth and everything that's in it,
And – which is more – you'll be a Man, my son!

This poem is simply saying, "Be consistent." However, understand that it is possible to be committed to something but not remain consistent in it. Commitment: means you have a passion to see it come to pass; consistency means that you will work dedicatedly to make it so.

If you possess commitment and consistency, then I guarantee you will have results – the three are synonymous when used in conjunction with one another. The Kipling poem gives credence to this in the second to last line: "Yours is the earth and everything in it." Results are fact-based accomplishments that your work renders, and if you have commitment, consistency, and results, then you will garner a seat at the table.

Doers want to see it done, and people always want to see what you do, not hear what you say. So, ironically, it's what you do that gives you a seat at the table and a voice, because your words are empty. People want to see what your life says, not just hear it.

What Privileges Does a Seat Give You?

As a United States citizen, you have certain inalienable rights. In the document called the Constitution of the United States of America, there is a list of laws called the Bill of Rights, which say that a naturalized citizen from birth has certain rights that cannot be forfeited. This document is part of what supposedly makes America the best country in the world and causes the rest of the world want to come and live here. This is called privilege, and it is not a right. Privilege is something that is usually earned. It is a special right, advantage, or immunity granted or available to a particular party or people. A seat at the table gives you access to privilege, and it allows you the ability to bypass certain processes. However, without equivocation, I want each of you to understand that privilege brings with it more responsibility and consequence than a right. The weight of privilege means that your actions, decisions, and mistakes are far more scrutinized than those of a person without a seat.

One who is given a seat should never take it for granted, because with it comes the responsibilities of representing and speaking on behalf of others. Have you ever been in a situation where someone was given the ability to speak on your behalf, and you gave them explicit instruction on how to vote for you, but they voted as they wished according to their own bias, and the results were not favorable for you? A seat at the table gives you a vote, but not many people realize how big a privilege the right to vote is.

During the time immediately following the end of slavery, it was determined that blacks would not be afforded the right to vote, and this practice was in place in the South until the 1960s. The thing is, in a democracy, the right to vote is the most important thing we possess. The reason is because voting has the ability to determine who is in power, and who has little voice at the table. That simply means who is in control of the House of Representatives and Senate, both in the federal government and at the state level.

The right to vote is so important that during the Civil Rights era, people literally fought, bled, and died for the privilege to vote. Sadly, even while most Americans are given a seat at the table because of the right to vote, many don't exercise it, because they feel that their vote will not make a difference. The privileges that a seat brings are numerous and undeniably valuable. However, the greatest privilege that a seat affords you is the ability to choose. Have you ever been in a predicament where your right to choose was hindered? Well, many places don't have that privilege, and without it, life can seem very hopeless.

What Responsibilities Does a Seat Bring?

Luke 12:48 says; "*For unto whomsoever much is given, of him shall be much required*" (KJV). I use this scripture reference in conjunction with a seat at the table because I don't want it to be misconstrued – with a seat comes great responsibility. As stated earlier, the seat is really not about your personal agenda. No, it is for the benefit of others, and for each seat you are afforded the opportunity to sit in, there come many attachments, commitments, and distractions that are connected to it. Most chairs have four legs attached to them, and the seat is supported by those legs. This is profound, because as just a seat is supported, so too is the figurative seat supported by four legs that it is accountable to: husbandry, fatherhood, service, and community activism.

A seat is usually given because those seated have noted that your life has spoken a certain tone and followed a specific path, and usually it is based upon family life and community service. The first tenet of family life is marriage, and the first ordination of marriage is husbandry. I use the term "husbandry" because it means "one who manages or oversees the management and the conservation of resources." There is no greater duty than that of a husband, because it is that which yields the greatest resources, and they are a wife and children. The apostle Paul gave a very compelling directive to the husband when he said, *"Husbands, love your wives, even as Christ also loved the church, and gave himself for it"* (Ephesians 5:25, KJV). A husband's first responsibility is love and selflessness. His calling is one of sacrifice, and of a whole investment to the building of his wife and children to their betterment.

The first tenet of husbandry is investment. When the term "investment" is used, it doesn't necessarily relate to finances; although financial investment is a necessary tool for family growth, the responsibility of sowing into your wife is the most mature, wise, and husbandly thing that a man can do. A woman or a wife has the ability to take whatever you give her and increase it, but understand that this is a two-way street, because whatever you sow into your wife, she will multiply. So, if you sow love, then you'll get love multiplied; if you sow groceries, then you'll get meals; if you sow your seed, then you'll reap a child. However, if you sow negativity, then you'll reap negativity; if you sow complacency, then you'll reap discontentment; if you sow insults and abuse, then you'll reap strife and contempt; and if you sow infidelity, then you'll reap divorce. A wife will increase whatever you sow into her. But remember, I said "a wife," not "a woman," because an ordinary woman does not a wife make. Know who you are joining into covenant with.

If God is blessing, and both husband and wife are fertile, then children will be born to a marriage. However intentional or unintentional the conception of a child may be, always remember that child rearing and fatherhood are done on purpose. There are two scriptures that come to mind when I think about fatherhood. The first is Proverbs 13:22, which says, *"A good man leaves an inheritance to his children's children: but the wealth of the sinner is laid up for the just"* (KJV2000). The second scripture is Psalm 127:3, and it reads, *"Children are an inheritance from the Lord. They are a reward from Him"* (GW).

It's notable that when the Word talks about children in these two scriptures, the word before and after "children" is "inheritance." What that says to me is that God is very purposeful about giving children, and what they should be given. I deem it safe to say that a person who squanders an inheritance is foolish. Well, if that's the case, then why not be intentional with what God deems as a reward?

Fatherhood is the most precious gift a man can be given, and the weightiest of responsibilities. Therefore, a man who seeks to be a good father had better stay rooted and grounded in the Word of God (Proverbs especially) and immersed in love. Love is the light that makes all things grow, but it's a misguided man who will make investments of himself, time, and love outside of his home. A wise and righteous man understands that "charity begins at home and spreads abroad." This was a saying that my mother would often say, so when I became a head football coach, it rang constantly in my ears. As a result, as much instructing, training, and love as I heaped on my players, I heaped it on my own children first, and I never made them feel like they were second fiddle to something that I did outside of our family.

Fatherhood will always be the scale by which every man is weighed. This, in my opinion, is the most important measure of a man, because although some experience marital break-ups, you never stop being a father and you never divorce your kids, regardless of what you may go through as a couple.

Community activism is critical in having a seat at the table extended to you. No matter what entity or endeavor you are adjoined to, if it involves the lives of others, it involves community, and therefore it requires you to be active. When the term "community activism" is thought of, many people think that it involves boycotts, picketing, and civil rights movements, but whatever you are involved in that affects the lives of others, it is your community, whether it be your block clubs, PTA/Local School Council, fraternal organization, church, etc.

All of these entities require active participation if you are to thrive and be successful. Most times, community activism will lead to one of two results: hatred or praise. If you aim to cause change through activism, you can expect resistance from the people who don't want change, and praise from the people who do, only if you are effective. In the movie *The Dark Knight*, District Attorney Harvey Dent said, "You either die a hero, or you live long enough to see yourself become the villain." This is true, and people who have fought to serve their communities have experienced both. Martyrs such as Dr. King, Medgar Evers, and dare I say Jesus Christ lived and effected enough change to die heroes. However, groups like the Black Panther Party were vilified by those who wanted the conditions of blacks to be stagnant.

Community activism, no matter how large or small, will cause you to be invited to the table. The key to success is, once you get a seat, you still have to remain active, because you never arrive. You should dictate that you work that much harder to ensure that your community thrives.

Matthew 20:26 says, "*Not so with you. Instead, whoever wants to become great among you must be your servant*" (NIV). These were the words of Jesus to His disciples. What He was trying to get them to understand was that greatness doesn't come by being served, it comes in the way of serving. Honor is found in serving, as it is stated by many who understand the esteem of servitude when they say, "It was an honor to serve you." The awesome thing is, to a true servant, it gives them pleasure to serve someone who may not have as high a station in life, but in serving with a gracious heart, that person can be made to feel like a king, and every now and then we all need to be made to feel special. Besides, if God is no respecter of a person, then why should you be?

Servitude is the highest form of respect one person can bestow upon another. By the esteem of the unlearned, it appears that servitude or serving is a low position and office. However, to the wise, it is understood that a servant is worth all that they are afforded in life. Without a servant, there is no king. So, the question is, who is more valuable? The heart of a servant will always be noticed before the desire of one to be served. The greatest esteem of any public official comes when it is deemed, whether while they're living or after they're dead, that they were a "great public servant." Jesus Himself washed the feet of His disciples, because He understood that if you don't have the humility to serve, then you will never possess the ability to lead.

No matter what office or station you attain, remember, if people are affected as a result of your being in said office, then you should always approach, address, and acknowledge it as a servant. People who serve others will always get the opportunity to do so, and that service will get them promotion. But know this: a person with a servant's heart, no matter how high up the ladder they climb, will always seek to serve. A person who always seeks to be served may get a seat at the table, but I guarantee that they will not stay seated. The greatest person in the world or at the table isn't the one who sits to be served. No, it's the one who comes up and smiles, and says "Can I take your order?" or "How can I serve you today?" Always remember that.

Chapter V

Knighthood

Knighthood is as old and respected an honor and position as men have known since medieval times. Being a knight wasn't only a position of honor, but it was a position of service. It was and still is a position of legacy, because knights produce knights. A knight's whole purpose was to serve and protect his lord or liege, and also to be skillful in warfare. In the subsequent sections, I will expound more on the duties, standards, and requirements of knighthood.

Taking on a New Title

Every boy is born with the ability to be a king inside of him. However, each and every man should aspire to have knightly qualities. A knight is the lowest ranking in the feudal system, but even so, the position of a knight was held in the highest regards by both royalty and commoner, because he lived, fought, and even died by a code of conduct that distinguished him from anyone above or beneath him in station. The title of knight was given only after specific mandates and requirements were met and completed. A knight was only dubbed or ordained after he had given years of service as a squire and had proven himself skillful in battle and loyal to his lord or liege.

A knight's life was one of service, chivalry, protection, and loyalty. Without these provable attributes, no squire became a knight. A knight was given a section of land to support himself and his family, but he was given far more privileges that afforded him a good life. Even though being a knight isn't an aspiration in today's time and society, it should be, because being knightly, or living by the code of a knight, is the noblest desire that a man can have. The reason for this is because being a knight is founded in servitude, but not slavery, and as Jesus said, a servant is the greatest of all men.

There are no kings, dukes, lords, or earls without the service of a knight, because not only does a knight serve his leader in loyalty, but a knight is the actual enforcer of a ruler's authority. Without the musketeers, King Louis XIII had no protection or power. Not only should a knight be a faithful and loyal servant, but he should be skilled in warfare as well.

I liken today's Secret Service detail of the President of the United States to the knights of old, and in the setting of the church, I would compare the Deacon Board to the knights of the pastor. Not every knight will not ascend to the throne; however, every knight can have knightly qualities. The same is said for a king: a good king should possess knightly qualities. He should be a servant of his people, be loyal to his court, possess chivalrous qualities, and be skilled in battle. When I say "skilled in battle," I don't mean a fighting man in the natural sense, but he should be able to protect his kingdom, both naturally and spiritually. Be he knight or king, a man of valor should know how to wage war for his subjects. Spiritual battles loom much larger than physical ones, especially in this day and time. If a man can't defend his land, people, or kingdom, then he isn't fit to be a knight or a king. As it was said previously, in order for someone to be dubbed a knight, they had to prove that they are proficient in battle. Well, spiritual warfare is the battleground of this day and age, and a man without skill in praying, spiritual warfare, and warring against demonic attacks against his family is no knight at all.

Kings and knights have been synonymous with each other for as long as there have been both. A great king wars with his army, such as King David did, and King Arthur as well. He also is a man of courage who does not cower from battle. A knight's job is to serve, protect, be loyal to, and honor his king. In taking on the title and vestments of knighthood, you are saying that you will not only serve the leaders you are under, but his people as well, and more importantly, you will live honorably before them with a code of chivalry – and that doesn't mean pulling out chairs. Are you ready for such a title, and do you have the wherewithal to do so? There was an old commercial that used to say, "Zenith, the quality goes in before the name goes on." It's the same for a knight.

1. Why Is a Title Bestowed?

Trust is the foundation of every title that's bestowed upon a man, whether it is president, pastor, general, deacon, team captain, doctor, or knight. It says that what you have lived, and the body of service (there goes that word again) that you have behind your name, states that you have been loyal in learning and following, and now you can be trusted to lead. Everything in this book has been written in conjunction with service and loyalty to a people, a process, and a purpose. The same is true in the bestowing of a title. A title simply says that you have satisfactorily satisfied a course or requirement, and now you can be trusted to fulfill the duties that the title brings.

In the swearing in of presidents and any other position that is given based upon the people's trust, a vow is taken, or an oath is made. Why? It's the same thing done when a person is given the title of a witness in a court of law. Many titles are given with a swearing in and a vow that says you will faithfully perform the duties of said office. Usually, a Bible is present, or the presence of God is invoked somewhere during the swearing in. This is because they are asking you to give your word, and the Bible is used to swear by because there is no greater or more binding word than the Word of God.

A title is bestowed because you have shown yourself to be faithful in service, competent in the commission of duties, skillful in performing, and loyal in the fulfillment of your obligations. This is especially true in assigning roles or promotions in public service positions such as police officers, firefighters, doctors, etc. This is because it is based on the public's trust that you hold their best interest at heart, and that their well-being and safety is held in higher regard than your own. That is why badges, emblems, and symbols are given, because they indicate that you stand behind an ideal and commitment that says you can be trusted.

The same is true for a knight. A knight's symbol was a coat of arms that he'd sworn allegiance to, or a suit of armor that he'd worn in battle. You never see people dressed as police officers who aren't. If someone does that, the offense is punishable by lengthy prison sentences. You have to be careful of a person who is always seeking a title, but never wants to fully commit to the obligations of that title or office. The same is true for someone who has a title but isn't worthy of it (like a certain former president of the United States). Title bestowment, especially when it relates to service and the protection of people, is very serious and should be earned. Otherwise, you're just impersonating whatever that title is, and the person that should have it. Are you okay with that?

2. The Requirements of Title Maintenance

The requirements of a knight are many, and yet at the same time, few. I say this because they are all intermingled in service, loyalty, and protection, and these are qualities that should be inherently present in every man who is called or qualified for knighthood. A knight should have qualities that are uncommon in most men but seem to be normal characteristics to him. That's because not every man is naturally meant to be a knight. However, every man can be taught to be a knight and trained to have knightly characteristics.

Every job has evaluations and performance critiques, and the same is true for knighthood, or acting as a knight. A man with knightly aspirations has a set of requirements that he must adhere to, because one's job performance must be verified. As I have stated and restated in this section, the first requirement for any knight or candidate for knighthood is service. If he has not been a servant, or has no record of service, then he is not qualified to be a knight. In the public school system, there is a requirement for graduation that you must accumulate Forty service learning hours, and they have to be verified and signed off by a teacher or a staff member. This is to ensure that you aren't just book smart, but that your high school career had some form of investment in the betterment of others. I for one applauded this initiative, because it mandated the need for students to understand that life isn't just about you.

The second requirement is loyalty. If a man has no loyalty grounded in him, nor does he act in loyalty to his leader or to a cause, then in fact, he is not a knight but a mercenary, and that is one who hires himself out for war to the highest bidder. Where no loyalty exists, treason is on the horizon. Next, if he is not prepared for battles nor engages in them, then he is not qualified, nor can he protect anyone's interests, including his own.

There are other virtues that should be continually displayed to ensure that a knightly title is maintained, or a position of honor is perpetuated. The following characteristics not only ensure that the title is maintained, but also qualify a man to become a knight:

1. Loyalty: Staying Faithful. *"For I delight in loyalty rather than sacrifice"* (Hosea 6:6, NASB).

2. Servant Leadership: Being Devoted. *"But whoever wishes to be great among you shall be your servant"* (Matthew 20:26, NASB).

3. Kindness: Treating Others Well. *"What is desirable in a man is his kindness"* (Proverbs 19:22, NASB).

4. Humility: Putting Others First. *"Do nothing from selfishness or empty conceit, but with humility... Regard*

one another as more important than yourselves" (Philippians 2:3, NASB).

5. Purity: Having a Clean Heart. *"Let no one look down on your youthfulness, but rather in speech, conduct, love, faith and purity, show yourself an example of those who believe"* (1 Timothy 4:12, NASB).

6. Honesty: Always Being Truthful. *"Therefore, laying aside falsehood, speak truth, each one of you, with his neighbor, for we are members of one another"* (Ephesians 4:25, NASB).

7. Self-Discipline: Being Like Jesus. *"Have nothing to do with worldly fables... discipline yourself for the purpose of godliness... Godliness is profitable for all things, since it holds a promise for the present life and also for the life to come"* (1 Timothy 4:7-8, NASB).

8. Excellence: Striving to Be the Best and Do the Best Job Possible. *"Do you not know that those who run in a race all run, but only one receives the prize? Run in such a way that you may win"* (1 Corinthians 9:24, NASB).

9. Integrity: Being Filled with Sincerity and Honesty. *"He who walks in integrity walks securely, but he who perverts his ways will be found out"* (Proverbs 10:9, NASB).

10. Perseverance: Staying with it. *"And let us not be weary in well doing, for in due season we shall reap, if we faint not"* (Galatians 6:9, KJV).

If a man possesses these character traits, then I guarantee he will always fulfill the duties of his calling to knighthood, and the maintenance of his title will always be in good standing.

3. Understanding What It Means to Bow and Rise

Each and every person on this planet has a trigger that will spark a flame of ire in them. Sometimes it's a person, and sometimes it's a thing, but whatever it is, we all have something that can irritate us to the point of losing our cool. There is no one born that is exempt from this human condition, not even Jesus. Jesus was as calm and collected as they come, but He was no pushover. He knew how to call you out on your mess with such humility, but He also knew how to set things straight when He knew that people were disrespectful to the things of God, and to God Himself. Sometimes, it is very necessary to swallow your pride and digress from situations for the greater good. However, sometimes it is necessary to show people that you mean business.

This is what I call understanding when to bow and rise. In history, wars have been averted because cooler heads prevailed. Yet there have also been times throughout history when leaders or countries had to show their strength. The noblest quality of a knight (in my estimation) is to know when to show humility and when to show force. Solomon said in Ecclesiastes that there is a time and season for everything. There is a time to fight, and a time for peace.

In the knighting process known as "dubbing," a knight must come before the person of authority, kneel, and bow his head. After his dubbing, he rises as a knight. First, he had to bow in submission to someone with authority over him, but after he rises, he has the power to protect. There will always be situations, conflicts, and struggles, both internally and externally, that will make you want to kill everybody and let the paramedics sort them out. But a true man of valor understands how to take pause and knows when it is in his best interest not to raise up, because a hasty decision can lead to disaster. It's easy to fight an opponent, especially when you are not fearful of him. However, it is far more difficult to show restraint and deference when everything in you wants to explode and show your strength. But true strength is found in restraint, and in who you are underneath.

I have two examples that I need to show to get my point home. The first is Superman. Superman is always Superman, but he humbles himself as Clark Kent. Although he takes abuse as Clark Kent, he only shows his strength when it is necessary to act. He always knows that he is capable of annihilating anybody and anything, but he shows restraint and humility, because he knows who he is. The Bible says in Proverbs 25:28, *"He that hath no rule over his own spirit is like a city that is broken down, and without walls"* (KJV). Translation: If you can't control yourself, then you will eventually crumble.

The next example is a skyscraper. A skyscraper is very tall and impressive, but its true strength is in its foundation, and then its frame. The steel underneath all of the glass and brick is what gives it its strength. Yet few people realize that there's a system of weights and pulleys that allows the skyscraper to bend and sway when winds and storms come. Although it is in a storm, it is not affected, because of what is underneath. There has to be a resolve in the knightly man that says, "Whether I have on armor, or show humility, I am a knight."

My dad, who is a retired police officer, once stopped some guys from robbing a store in my community. His name was in the paper, and the story was on the radio. Needless to say, I was very proud. The thing was my dad was off duty when he apprehended the robbers. I asked my dad why he did it, especially when he was off duty, and he told me, "Whether I am on duty or off, I am a police officer twenty-four hours a day." No matter what the storm or test, or whether you bow or rise in the face of a situation, you are always being scrutinized, and because of that, your life is always serving as an example.

I recall seeing a movie when I was a kid. It was called *Angels with Dirty Faces*, and it starred James Cagney and Pat O'Brien. Cagney was a gangster and O'Brien was a priest, and they were best friends growing up. Well, there was a group of kids who idolized Cagney's character because he was tough. Ultimately, Cagney killed a cop and was sentenced to death. O'Brien asked him to play the role of a coward before he was executed, but he refused. But as he was being led to the electric chair, he put on an act, because he knew that if he hadn't, then the kids would have emulated his life, and he didn't want that. So, instead of going out a tough guy, he went out as a coward to save the lives of those kids. He knew that bowing would save lives, and rising would only benefit his ego, but in actuality, in his bowing, he had never risen so high. Understand what is at stake when you bow or rise, and how it will affect not only your life but the lives of others, and you could very well save a few along the way.

4. The Duties of a Knight

The duties of a knight were few, but they were extremely important, as they still are today. A knight's first duty was to serve his lord, or the one who made him a knight, and the same is true today. As a knightly man, you have a mandate to serve, and to ensure that another man's vision flourishes as you cultivate your own. If you aren't in service, or committed to serving someone, then you don't have knightly qualities, and you are ensuring that your own vision will never come to pass, because once again, if you don't know how to follow, then you will never know how to lead. Also, no matter how much elevation or promotion you receive, always make sure that you serve someone else, because you never arrive, and you are always accountable for making sure that someone else's vision thrives.

Next, you're assigned to be a protector, whether you are a knight in the service of a king, your church, or your community. You are called to be a protector whether it's property, souls, or making sure your neighborhood is safe. You are a protector. You should be loyal, and always make sure that people's backs are covered, be it through information, prayer, or keeping a watchful eye. In knighthood, there is no such thing as a "don't snitch, don't tell" rule, because that's the code of cowards.

Next, you have a duty to be an example. Someone should see your life and want to be like you. You should always set the tone for how to act, how to serve, how to dress, and how to lead. Intermingled with that, you should always be a replicator, or a mentor for others to learn the ways of valor.

Jesus said, "*No good tree bears bad fruit, nor does a bad tree bear good fruit. Each tree is recognized by its own fruit*" (Luke 6:43-44, NIV). The same is said for life. No one worth their salt leaves this earth without ever duplicating themselves in someone else. I mean, criminals train criminals. So, wouldn't it be fair to say that a knightly man should create a knightly man? The story of Jesus and the fig tree stands out here. Jesus was walking with his disciples and saw a fig tree, but upon reaching it, they saw that it had no fruit on it. So, Jesus cursed the tree, and basically said, "You won't fool anyone else." Well, upon returning, they saw that the tree had withered and died. Such is one who says he is a knight and doesn't produce knights. You will wither and die, having left nothing that anyone else can live off of. It is your duty to duplicate yourself in someone. If not, then you will be cursed.

Chapter VI

Squires

Making Squires

"Train up a child in the way he should go and
when he is old, he will not depart from it."
(Proverbs 22:6, KJV)

This is the basis upon which every child should be raised, not only boys, but girls as well. Training a child is not the same as teaching a child. Notice, the beginning of the scripture says; "Train up a child..." – it didn't say "teach." Training means to be in line with a set regiment or discipline, or to become proficient in the learning of a set job or skill. Teaching, on the other hand, means to instill the learning of a theory. Traditionally, an education is that which reinforces knowledge in that which you already have a foundation. Thus, to be trained in something means you have not only been taught about a thing, but you have been immersed in preparation to become that thing by title.

This is the case in making and training squires. A squire is a young man who is acting as an attendant to a knight before becoming a knight himself. Being a squire is a necessary cog if knighthood is to continue. Squires don't just become knights or acquire knightly behavior. No, a squire is trained to become a knight, and to live by and display a knightly existence. The problem is, in this day and time, immediate self-gratification is the "soup of the day." No one wants to go through the process to become changed anymore, and very few want to go through the process of training young men to change.

There is much to be said about the resolve of a drill sergeant, because he or she will go through the process of taking young, immature, unconfident, and undisciplined people and turning them into soldiers, over and over again. The thing about siring a squire is that it's usually one on one, and what that squire becomes is a direct reflection of the knight who trained him. Although a squire may have or be exposed to other trainers, ultimately, it is the responsibility of a knight to ensure that his squire is thorough and entire in all aspects of knighthood. Thus, the need for patience is paramount for both the knight and the squire.

The making of a squire is tedious work, and the painstakingly slow process is remarkably slower. However, a man or knight who trains a squire does so with the understanding of what is at stake. A doctor who trains a medical student does so with the understanding of the Hippocratic Oath that all doctors must vow upon completion of their studies, and that oath is: "First, do no harm." That oath doesn't apply only to patients, but also to the instructors training the doctors who treat patients. There is no circumventing of the process, and the same should be said in the training of a squire. Every noble profession is one entrenched in service, and especially that of the knighthood calling. Before a squire is taught to fight, he is taught how to serve, because in understanding service, he knows the very reason he becomes a knight, and what he is fighting for.

Selecting Squires: What Makes a Good Candidate?

"My sacrifice, O God, is a broken spirit; a broken and contrite heart you, God, will not despise."
(Psalm 51:17, NIV)

The first thing you should look for in a squire candidate is humility. Humility is the first characteristic in determining how big something or someone can grow. Proverbs 1:5 says, "A wise man shall hear and shall be wiser, and he that understands shall possess governments" (DRB). A young man who is eager to learn and be taught can be trained, and his potential to be great is limitless. A young man with a humble spirit will trust what his training is, and though he may ask questions, his questions are for knowledge and understanding, and not from a challenging and know-it-all perspective.

Most good candidates come from homes where love and structure are in abundance. However, that isn't always the case. Some of my greatest success stories as a coach are of young men who didn't have structure, visible love, or a father present in the home. However, they all had a willingness to learn, be trained, and be poured into, and not just in sports, but about manhood, fatherhood, service, humility, perseverance, and most importantly, is love. Though it may have been tough at times, it was worth it.

People, especially kids, know the difference between toleration and celebration. The key to discerning if they can be a quality squire is to see how they handle discipline, instruction, and correction. If they can be corrected and or disciplined, and come back the next day, then they have the makings of a good candidate. Proverbs 1:7 says, *"The fear of the Lord is the beginning of knowledge, but fools despise wisdom and instruction"* (NIV). If they can't stand to be instructed, then they will not be good candidates.

Some people think eagerness is a good measuring stick to determine if someone will be a good candidate, and that may be true. But I say that motive is a better measuring tool. Some people show eagerness and enthusiasm for something in the beginning, because they are looking at how it will benefit them, and not from a servant's heart, or how they can be seen or viewed by others for doing it. The method of separating the wheat from the tares is this: don't let them be seen doing anything until some time has passed, and if they are still eager and enthusiastic, then they are good ground to sow into.

Some young men don't know that they are or can't see themselves as potential candidates for knighthood. It is up to the knightly to recognize the qualities, and not leave the young man to his own devices. The same can be said for some adult men. Some men grow up without a role model/ mentor, but you can tell when a man is a good person, or has good character, but it just hasn't been cultivated within him. Therefore, it is up to you to go to him, and offer him training in the path of the knightly, because you are never too young or too old to walk in knighthood.

The Investment Benefits You More Than the Candidate

> "But we were gentle among you, even as a nurse
> cherishes her children: So being affectionately
> desirous of you, we were willing to have imparted
> unto you, not the gospel of God only, but also our
> own souls, because you were dear unto us."
>
> (1 Thessalonians 2:7-8, KJV2000)

Impartation is the most important tool for growth that there is. Any person who gains anything in life and doesn't impart, invest, or instill into the life of someone else will die unfulfilled and cursed. As I was having my Sunday dinner about four days ago, I was reflecting over my life and the word that my Apostle Dr. Matthew L. Stevenson III gave to the church. Basically, he was saying that if you haven't sown into anyone else, then you really can't expect your dream and aspirations to come to pass. So, at the service and after I had gotten home, I was asking God whether I had sown into the lives of others with all that I've had. Well, I thought about my coaching career and my church, but those are two things that I do effortlessly, so that really wasn't something that I considered a sacrifice, because I love doing them both.

Well, I got an inbox from a good friend of mine, and he said to call him, as he now lives in another state. I called him, and he told me that God had blessed him tremendously, and that when he was at his lowest, I had invested a bed and a place to stay without charge, and words that changed his life. My sowing into him changed his life, and now he was living a life that he had only dreamed about. Well, after I had stopped being a blubbering mess and gained my composure, I worshipped God, because He had let me know that He was pleased with me, but more than that, my life has had meaning, purpose, and made a difference in someone else's life.

Purpose is the very reason that God creates any of us, and though you may never know exactly what that purpose is, God is gracious and benevolent enough to show us bits and pieces of it. A life without purpose is a wasted life, and as I said in the previous chapters, if you haven't duplicated yourself, then you are cursed. A tree that never has its fruit harvested doesn't yield more or bigger fruit, but one that is harvested regularly continues to bear more and bigger fruit. If you don't invest in the lives of others, then you will become unfruitful, and the only thing you will be any good for will be firewood. Proverbs 27:17 says, "As *iron sharpens iron, so one person sharpens another*" (NIV). In investing, pouring into, imparting, or sharpening someone else, you are simultaneously reinvigorating your own life. Just as a battery is recharged by a running engine, a person's life is enhanced by imparting into another, especially the young. I swear to you, knowing that you have made someone else's life better, because you sowed into them, gives you an unexplainable sense of purpose. It is when your purpose is fulfilled that you will hear God say, "Well done, thou good and faithful servant," and that will be both in heaven and on earth.

Why Is It Necessary to Make Squires?

"While the earth remains, seedtime and harvest, cold and heat, summer and winter, day and night, shall not cease." (Genesis 8:22, ESV)

It will always be necessary to make squires, because it will always be necessary to have knights. The scripture that I used to start this segment spoke of the earth remaining, seedtime and harvest, and weather and seasons, and just like there is a natural process of the earth, there is a natural process of earthlings.

There will always be inhabitants on the earth, as long as the planet exists, and because of that, there will always be a need to sow and reap. This is true for people, because as long as the circle of life continues, people will be born, people will live, and people will grow old and eventually die. As people, we go through seasons and processes, and any time the processes of a species stop, it becomes extinct. There is a saying, "Youth must be served," and that is highly accurate, because the old can't do what they used to be able to, and they need the young to carry on. That's why new trees and fields are planted, livestock is raised, and squires are made.

If the knightly don't create squires, then a way of life, a system of values, and a legacy of pride through service and honor will die. So, with the world being in the shape it's in, we need an assembly line of squires, and truth be told, knights as well.

There is no way that I can do what I did as a twenty or thirty-year-old man. Neither my body nor my mind reacts the way it once did, and it becomes more and more obvious that time is no longer my ally. Therefore, the making of squires and teaching the next generations is of great importance, because the world is not the world that I grew up in, sadly. The morals and values that I held so dear are becoming extinct, and some have already done so. Ephesians 5:16 says that we should be *"redeeming the time, because the days are evil"* (KJV). This is the bitter truth.

In a time where the most coveted office in the world was occupied until recently by a person who openly lies, slanders and degrades women and the handicapped, and even condones groping women, then making more squires is vitally necessary, because if men don't stand up in and for righteousness, then men of unrighteous character will, and already have. The knightly men of valor are an old and dying breed, and if we don't develop a campaign of reinvigoration for the spirit of knighthood and the making of squires, then the knight and his knightly values will become as the dinosaur, extinct.

The Life You Live Before Your Squire

> *"You are the light of the world. A city set on a hill cannot be hidden; nor does anyone light a lamp and put it under a basket, but on the lampstand, and it gives light to all who are in the house. Let your light shine before men in such a way that they may see your good works, and glorify your Father who is in heaven."* (Matthew 5:14-16, NASB)

I've heard it said that "image is everything," and this holds some validity, especially in the eyes of a mentee. It is very important for a mentor to present the right image before his squire/mentee, because what that young man sees, he will eventually become. It's no different than how God created us in His image and in His likeness. The apostle Paul took it a step further, as it is proven in 2 Corinthians 3:18, which reads, "And we all, with unveiled face, continually seeing as in a mirror the glory of the Lord, are progressively being transformed into His image from glory to glory, which comes from the Lord, the Spirit" (AMP).

What this is saying is that whatever image is put before us on a continuous basis, we progressively become. Living the right life in front of your squire teaches them far more than your training sessions and teachings will, because even from birth, we are taught to walk, speak, and talk by example. The biggest lie or excuse of unaccountability is these words: "Do as I say, not as I do."

It is impossible to teach someone to walk if all they ever see you do is hop. Every move that you make is being recorded in the minds of those you mentor. If all a child sees growing up is inconsistency in lifestyles, then they will develop inconsistent character. If a boy sees his dad abuse and mistreat women all his life, then the odds are he will do the same, unless a strong example enters his life and changes his perspective.

Perspective, simply put, is a person's point of view, and how they perceive or look at someone or something. People's perspectives are usually formed by what they witness growing up, and what they are told on a consistent or inconsistent basis. Unless and until one's perspective is changed, the way they look at things is usually the way their parents saw them. All the evils in the world are in existence because of bad perspective. All forms of bigotry, prejudice, racism, even chauvinism is learned behaviors. No child starts off with these traits, and they only manifest because of what was lived before them.

Which brings me to my next point, and that is accountability. Every parent, mentor, teacher, pastor or anyone with influence should acquaint themselves with this word. In short, accountability is just saying that you take responsibility for your actions and their consequences. Here's a transparency... wait a minute, I just got a revelation. "Transparency" is derived from the word "transparent." According to Webster's Dictionary, "transparent" means "(of a material or article) allowing light to pass through so that objects behind can be distinctly seen." The operative word in that combined word is "parent," and the functioning verb in that definition is "light pass through." That definition says it all.

However, let me return to my original thought. I was having a talk with a parent, and he said that he was disappointed in how his six sons had turned out. He said that in spite of each of them having had tremendous gifts, abilities, and potential, he felt that each of them had failed as adults. Well, being familiar with the dynamic of that family, I made this observation. I said, "As a coach, it is my goal and responsibility to help each player reach their optimum potential, and to get that team to the championship and win it, especially if I have a team full of gifted players. If I fail to help them reach their pinnacle, then it wasn't their fault as players, it was my fault as a coach."

Every man who teaches a boy is responsible and accountable to that boy, to make sure that everything the boy sees is a shining example of knightly character and manhood that should make him want to duplicate the things he saw. Hopefully, they are good things, but that determination ultimately is yours, because good or bad, he will emulate and imitate what he has seen lived out before him. The question is, will you be a heroic monument of knighthood, or a stumbling block of great offense? The decision is yours, but first ask yourself this question: "Is the life that I live worth the life that will be lived out as a result of it?" Survey says...

Taking Squires to the Next Level

"Not as though I had already attained, either were already perfect: but I follow after, if that I may apprehend that for which I am apprehended of Christ Jesus.... But this one thing I do, forgetting those things which are behind, and reaching forth unto those things which are before, I press toward the mark of the prize of the high calling of God in Christ Jesus." (Philippians 3:12-14, KJV)

I have stated in several sections and chapters that everything is about accessing and achieving your next level. The only way you can mark your progress is by growth, and whatever that growth area may be, marking it is necessary. You never arrive, you never say "Soul, take thy rest," and you should never be satisfied with the current version of yourself, because you can always be better. We are called by God to go from level to level, glory to glory, and faith to faith. The apostle Paul is saying in the opening scripture that you can never rest on your past accomplishments, because there is no perfecting in your past, but only in your press towards your future. "Complacency breeds mediocrity, and mediocrity breeds failure" is a phrase that I pinned for my players, it was done to instill in them that you should never be satisfied with average when greatness is attainable. You should always instill this lesson in your squires repeatedly.

Those squired, especially boys of younger age, have a tendency to hang their hats on their "Eureka moment" – the moment when the light comes on, and they "get it." But be careful, because if they are allowed to stay in that place, then that will be all they get. In instructing your squires, remember that life is not just a bunch of periods, but a series of commas, which indicate, "Wait, there's more to this." When I was a teenager, we would gather in my neighborhood to shoot basketball at the local park, and there were two sides of the court, one deemed the kids' side, for the not-so-good players, and the other being the grown-up/hoopers' side. Well, me being me, I only had aspirations to play on the "A side," but I had to work on my game. So, every chance I got, I did, until one day, they let me play on the grown-up side. Needless to say, I was never satisfied playing on the kids' side again.

As a mentor training squires, you have to do whatever it takes to get him to be the best him that he can be. This is done by always presenting tests that challenge his resolve, because if his resolve isn't challenged, then the only thing left to do is dissolve. Paul said, "I press toward the mark for the prize." That in itself is an awesome analogy, because anything worth having is considered a prize, and has to be thought of as such, whether a squire is trained by competition against others, or he has to learn to press and conquer whatever stands in the way of his next level, including himself.

A squire should also be taught that while in pursuit of the next level, he should always pay attention to the journey and the process, because it is very possible that he may have to repeat it one day, and if he is a person that is set on attaining next levels, then he will. It may not be the exact same thing, but the steps are always similar. It's like doing math, because when you start off, it's simple addition, but it builds, and no matter how advanced it gets, it's always based on 1+1=2.

This is a poem that you should learn for yourself, and whenever you squire someone, they should commit it to memory as a tool for next-level training.

"See It Through"
by Edgar Albert Guest

When you're up against a trouble, meet it squarely face to face

Lift your chin and set your shoulders, plant your feet and take a brace.

When it's vain to try to dodge it, do the best that you can do

You may fail, but you may conquer, see it through!

Black may be the clouds about you and your future may seem grim,

But don't let your nerve desert you; keep yourself in fighting trim.

If the worst is bound to happen, spite of all that you can do,

Running from it will not save you, see it through!

Even hope may seem but futile, when with troubles you're beset,

But remember you are facing just what other men have met.

You may fail, but fail still fighting; don't give up, what er' you do;

Eyes front, head high to the finish. See it through!

The Insurance of Continued Legacy

"And the things that thou hast heard of me among many witnesses, the same commit thou to faithful men, who shall be able to teach others also."

(2 Timothy 2:2, KJV)

It's funny how our plans are never God's plans, and as it says in 1 Corinthians 13:9, "Now our knowledge is partial and incomplete, and even the gift of prophecy reveals only part of the whole picture" (NLT). I say this to say that when the idea of the "King's Cupboard" came to me, I only saw it as a clothing line, because the brothers at the ministry I attend would often come up and say to me, "Elder Elray, you need to do a class on teaching men how to dress." I concurred and thought about how and what I would teach, and also develop a clothing line in the process.

Now, the thought of imparting into men about life and how to navigate it was always in me, and actually, I had already planned on having a few brothers from the ministry come by my home and fellowship as we talked about different things. You see, I am a coach, and nothing gives me greater pleasure than to see the lives of boys and young men changed for the better. Well, as I was doing my business plan, I heard God say, "If you have a car that looks good on the outside, but has a bad motor, then it's a lemon. So, if you have men dressed up, and their hearts and minds are messed up, then it's like gift wrapping garbage, and you're perpetrating a fraud. I need my men whole!" Thus, he gave me the layout and outline for *The King's Cupboard*.

As it was stated in the vision statement of this road map to destiny, *The King's Cupboard* was designed to ensure that a legacy is left behind that will shape and grow a fundamental heritage of pride, honor, and dignity not only through precepts and examples, but through the life-fortifying concept of service. This book/training manual of sorts was not my idea, but God's, and it was only done by His inspiration and to give Him glory. I would like to acknowledge that there are quite a few repetitive statements, quotes, and scriptures in this book, but it was done with the thought in mind that the only way that you assimilate anything as a habit is through repetition – remember, I am a coach.

The desired legacy of *The King's Cupboard* is to make sure that each one would teach one, and more importantly, teach one properly, because the only way that you can truly change and empower a people is through knowledge, and truly, knowledge is power. Everything starts with a foundation for legacy, and the foundation for *The King's Cupboard* is information. First of all, the initiative is built on purpose, because where purpose is not known, abuse is inevitable. However, purpose with missing steps can never be fulfilled. This is why it is necessary to be thorough in dissemination of information, and that we cover all steps, because I have learned through a communication exercise that if instruction isn't clear and concise from person to person, then by the time it gets to the end, it isn't the same message.

The way the legacy of *The King's Cupboard* is ensured is to make sure that it isn't just taught to young men and boys, but that the men teaching it are living it as well, and that their lives are their words, and that kingship and knighthood and all the tenets that they possess are actually a way of life.

It is necessary, and it has to be more than words on a page or a book on a shelf, because it is very easy to forget what you've read, but it is impossible to forget what you live. And if that is the mission, then the teaching and instruction found in this book will never die, because just as a boy imitates his father shaving, he will imitate his living, and that's what we hope.

In conclusion, I pray that this manual has blessed you and inspired you to grow daily as a king, and to live a life of knightly character, but even more, that it mandates a desire within you to create that growth and character in the young men in your life. I want to leave you with this charge. Become the king and the knight in this book, and don't miss or skip any steps, because someone will be watching your every move. So, at the end of the day, become this book, and be aware that someone is reading you every day, and the life of the one who is reading your story depends on what you are writing. Thank you!